THE WORLD

Mathematics
Revision

Gillian Rich and Fiona Mapp

Contents

What's the point?

Fred wants to build a new bookshelf in his bedroom. He needs to work out how long the shelf needs to be so that all his books will fit.

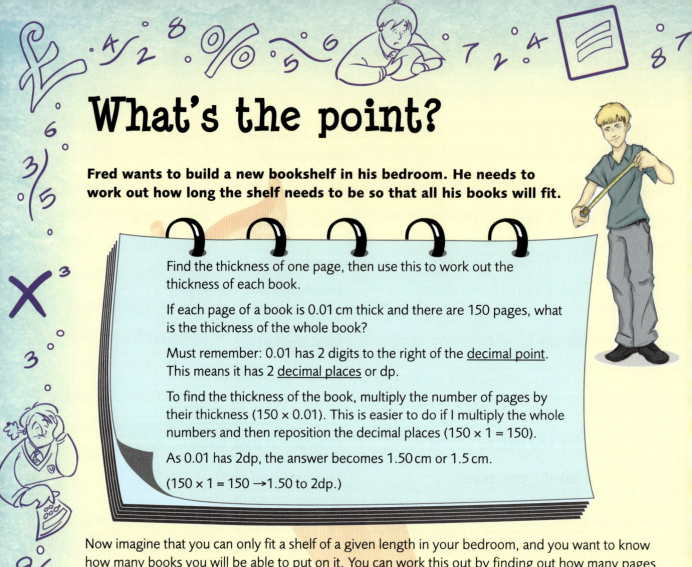

Find the thickness of one page, then use this to work out the thickness of each book.

If each page of a book is 0.01 cm thick and there are 150 pages, what is the thickness of the whole book?

Must remember: 0.01 has 2 digits to the right of the <u>decimal point</u>. This means it has 2 <u>decimal places</u> or dp.

To find the thickness of the book, multiply the number of pages by their thickness (150 × 0.01). This is easier to do if I multiply the whole numbers and then reposition the decimal places (150 × 1 = 150).

As 0.01 has 2dp, the answer becomes 1.50 cm or 1.5 cm.

(150 × 1 = 150 →1.50 to 2dp.)

Now imagine that you can only fit a shelf of a given length in your bedroom, and you want to know how many books you will be able to put on it. You can work this out by finding out how many pages will fit on the shelf by dividing its length by the thickness of one page.

For example, if your shelf were 1.5 metres long, how many pages would fit on the shelf?

Make sure that both measurements are in the same unit. (The shelf length is in metres and the thickness of each page in centimetres, so change the metres to centimetres before you start your calculations.)

There are 100 cm in 1 m, so 1.5 m equals 150 cm. (1.5 cm × 100 = 150 cm)

Divide the length of the shelf by the thickness of one page to find the number of pages that will fit. (This is easier to do if you divide by a whole number, in this case by 1.)

To change 0.01 to 1 means the position of the decimal point moves 2 places to the right. To keep the balance of the original division, you need to do the same to the 150, so this becomes 15 000. (150 ÷ 0.01 → 150/0.01 = 15 000/1 = 15 000

You now want to know how many books will fit on the shelf. If each book has 250 pages, you can divide 15 000 by 250 and find that 60 books fit on the shelf because 15 000 ÷ 250 = 60.

12

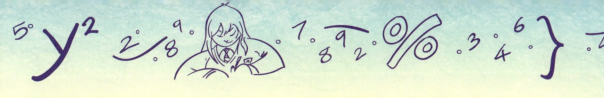

Match up

1 Match each of these books to the correct thickness.

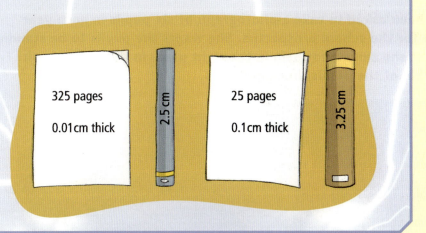

325 pages
0.01 cm thick

2.5 cm

25 pages
0.1 cm thick

3.25 cm

2 You want a shelf for your computer manuals. You have room for a shelf that is one metre long. The average page thickness of your manuals is 0.01 cm and the average number of pages in a manual is 850. Complete this chart.

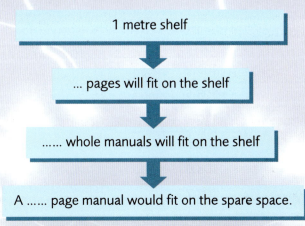

1 metre shelf

↓

... pages will fit on the shelf

↓

...... whole manuals will fit on the shelf

↓

A ...... page manual would fit on the spare space.

· TOP TIPS ·

When working a practical problem, always ask yourself if the answer makes sense.

KEY FACTS

⬆ **Always make sure that the units of measurement are the same before calculating a problem.**

➡ **Multiplying by 100 has the effect of moving the decimal point 2 places to the right, and dividing by 100 has the effect of moving the decimal point 2 places to the left. Of course the decimal point can't really move, it is the digits that can. However, as it looks as though the decimal point moves, it's quite a good way to think of it.**

⬆ **When counting decimal places, count from the decimal point to the right.**

⬅ **After multiplication, when replacing decimal places in an answer, start counting from the extreme right-hand digit.**

5

Reach for the heights

A photographer has been asked to take a photograph of six pupils in each year group in Key Stage 3 for the school prospectus. She wants the pupils to be standing in height order so that she can stand them in the right place in the photograph. The table shows the heights of the pupils, in centimetres.

Y7	Y8	Y9
86.25	94.5	109.9
83.05	94.05	108.5
83.1	91.75	110
89	91	108.55
83.25	94.55	108.03
85	94.25	108.7

Help the photographer put the pupils in <u>ascending</u> height order (so that the shortest is first).

To put decimals in order:

1 Look at the whole numbers before the decimal point (start with the smallest number, as the heights are to be placed in ascending order, and use the symbols <, ≤, ≥, > (see Key Facts on page 7) for clearer working.

2 Look at the first decimal place (tenths $\frac{1}{10}$) (if these are the same, compare the second decimal place (hundredths $\frac{1}{100}$) and so on).

The order then becomes:
height ≤ 90 cm: 83.05 cm, 83.1 cm, 83.25 cm, 85 cm, 86.25 cm, 89 cm
90 cm < height ≤ 100 cm: 91 cm, 91.75 cm, 94.05 cm, 94.25 cm, 94.5 cm, 94.55 cm
height >100 cm: 108.03 cm, 108.5 cm, 108.55 cm, 108.7 cm, 109.9 cm, 110 cm

12

Order, order!

1 Put each of these sets of measurements in ascending order. (All are measured in centimetres.)

a)

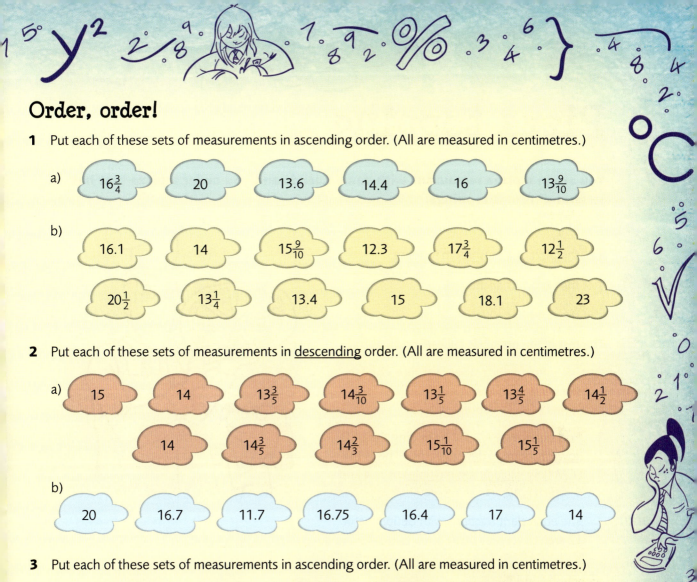

$16\frac{3}{4}$ 20   13.6   14.4   16 $13\frac{9}{10}$

b)

16.1   14 $15\frac{9}{10}$ 12.3 $17\frac{3}{4}$ $12\frac{1}{2}$

$20\frac{1}{2}$ $13\frac{1}{4}$ 13.4   15   18.1   23

2 Put each of these sets of measurements in <u>descending</u> order. (All are measured in centimetres.)

a)

15   14 $13\frac{3}{5}$ $14\frac{3}{10}$ $13\frac{1}{5}$ $13\frac{4}{5}$ $14\frac{1}{2}$

14    $14\frac{3}{5}$ $14\frac{2}{3}$ $15\frac{1}{10}$ $15\frac{1}{5}$

b)

20   16.7   11.7   16.75   16.4   17   14

3 Put each of these sets of measurements in ascending order. (All are measured in centimetres.)

20.25   20.1   20.275   20.05   20.075

KEY FACTS

⬆ < means less than and ≤ means less than or equal to.

⬆ > means more than and ≥ means more than or equal to.

⬆ If ordering <u>fractions</u>, either change into decimals by dividing numerator by denominator and use the method on page 6, or use <u>equivalent fractions</u> (see page 8).

⬆ To change a decimal to a fraction:

   a) use the digits to the right of the decimal point as the numerator

   b) the denominator is 1 with a zero for each digit in the numerator, e.g. $0.237 = \frac{237}{1000}$

   c) always give a fraction in its lowest terms, e.g. $0.275 = \frac{275}{1000} = \frac{11}{40}$

· TOP TIPS ·

1 When arranging items in ascending order, start with the smallest and finish with the largest.

2 When arranging items in descending order, start with the largest and finish with the smallest.

3 Take care when ordering negative numbers, e.g. −2.35 > −2.475 and −5.5 < 1.25

Pizza topping

You are in a pizza restaurant with some friends and you order a pizza that has several different toppings.

$\frac{1}{3}$ of the pizza has mushroom topping.

$\frac{1}{4}$ of the pizza has anchovies.

$\frac{1}{6}$ of the pizza has olives.

The rest of the pizza has cheese topping.

One of your friends does not like cheese, so you want to know what fraction of the pizza has cheese topping.

1. Add together $\frac{1}{3} + \frac{1}{4} + \frac{1}{6}$ by finding the LCD (<u>lowest common denominator</u>). This is the LCM (<u>lowest common multiple</u>) of 3, 4 and 6, which is 12.

   The equivalent fractions with denominator 12 are:

   $\frac{4}{12}$, $\frac{3}{12}$ and $\frac{2}{12}$:

   Add these up:

   $\frac{4}{12} + \frac{3}{12} + \frac{2}{12} = \frac{9}{12}$

   The cheese topping covers $1 - \frac{9}{12} = \frac{12}{12} - \frac{9}{12} = \frac{3}{12}$.

2. As 3 is a <u>common factor</u> of 3 and 12, simplify or cancel $\frac{3}{12}$ into its lowest terms by dividing numerator and denominator by 3. **This gives an answer of $\frac{1}{4}$.**

Several people don't like anchovies, so you want to know what <u>percentage</u> of the pizza does not have anchovies.

1. Anchovies cover $\frac{1}{4}$ of the pizza, so $\frac{3}{4}$ of the pizza does not have anchovies.

2. To change this to a percentage, multiply by 100.

   $\frac{3}{4} \times 100 = \textbf{75\%}$

12

What do you need?

You will find the answers to the questions below in this pizza. Write down the letter corresponding to each answer in the order of the questions. Your letters should make the name of something you need when you cancel fractions.

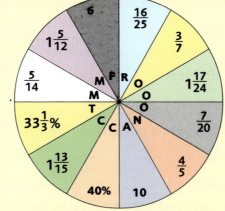

1. Phil is starving. He eats $\frac{2}{3}$ of a cheese and tomato pizza and $\frac{1}{5}$ of a mushroom pizza. When he has finished, he eats another whole mushroom pizza that he finds in the kitchen. How much does he eat in total?

2. Naomi eats $\frac{3}{4}$ of a salami pizza, $\frac{1}{8}$ of a mushroom pizza plus $\frac{5}{6}$ of a cheese and olive pizza. How much does she eat in total?

3. A dog likes to sneak into the kitchen and eat pizza when no one is looking.

   2 pizzas and $\frac{2}{3}$ of another one are left on the table and the dog eats 1 whole pizza and $\frac{1}{4}$ of another. How much is left?

4. A dog eats half of a salami pizza. There had been $\frac{6}{7}$ of it left on the table. How much is left when the dog has finished?

5. The same dog eats half of the $\frac{6}{7}$ of another salami pizza. How much is left?

6. One night, Dave feels hungry. He looks in the fridge and sees one whole cheese and tomato pizza and one fifth of another one. He eats two-thirds of these. How much is left in the fridge?

7. If $\frac{3}{4}$ of a pizza is left, how many people can eat an $\frac{1}{8}$ slice?

8. If $2\frac{1}{2}$ pizzas are left, how many people can eat a $\frac{1}{4}$ slice?

9. What percentage is $\frac{2}{5}$ of a pizza?

10. What percentage is $\frac{1}{3}$ of a pizza?

11. What fraction is 35% of a pizza?

12. What fraction is 64% of a pizza?

   The mystery name is: ....

KEY FACTS

⬆ When you add and subtract fractions, first find a common denominator.

➡ When you multiply fractions, change all mixed numbers into improper fractions, then multiply across top and bottom.

⬇ When you divide fractions, change all mixed numbers into improper fractions, then turn the second fraction upside down and multiply across top and bottom.

⬆ To change a fraction to a percentage, multiply by 100.

⬅ To change a percentage to a fraction, put it over 100 and simplify to its lowest terms.

• TOP TIPS •

1. It is usual to give fraction answers in lowest terms. (See the working for the cheese topping on the pizza.)

2. You should also turn all improper fraction answers into mixed numbers.

3. 'of' in a calculation is replaced by 'times' or 'multiplied by'.

Test your knowledge 1

1 Fill the gaps in the calculations below.

a) $4 \times$ .... $= 0.04$ b) $7.2 \div$ .... $= 72$

c) $45 \div$ .... $= 4500$ d) $5.1 \times$ .... $= 0.0051$

e) $0.72 \times$ .... $= 720$ f) .... $\div 0.1 = 56$

g) .... $\div 0.001 = 57$ h) .... $\times 0.01 = 63$

(8 marks)

2 Harry and James each bought a pizza. Harry ate $\frac{4}{5}$ of his. James ate $\frac{5}{6}$ of his. Who has more left?

(2 marks)

....

3 Put these fractions in order, from the smallest to largest.

$\frac{4}{7}, \frac{13}{21}, \frac{19}{42}, \frac{1}{3}, \frac{4}{5}$ ....

(2 marks)

4 During a javelin competition, the distances thrown were as follows.

Student	Distance the javelin was thrown (in metres)
Chloe	8.160
Hussain	8.280
Emily	7.260
Matthew	8.090
Jessica	8.281

Arrange the distances in order of size, smallest distance first.

Distances in ascending order

(2 marks)

5 The table below shows some equivalent fractions and percentages. Complete the table.

Fraction	Percentage
$\dfrac{3}{5}$	
$\dfrac{1}{8}$	
	45%
	62%

(4 marks)

6 Calculate these:

a) $\dfrac{4}{7} + \dfrac{2}{14} =$

b) $\dfrac{1}{12} + \dfrac{2}{3} =$

c) $3\dfrac{3}{5} + 1\dfrac{2}{9} =$

d) $\dfrac{11}{12} - \dfrac{1}{4} =$

e) $4\dfrac{5}{9} - 1\dfrac{1}{3} =$

f) $\dfrac{4}{5} - \dfrac{1}{7} =$

(6 marks)

7 A hockey team won $\dfrac{2}{5}$ of their games and lost $\dfrac{1}{4}$ of them.

What fraction of their games did they draw?

(2 marks)

(Total 26 marks)

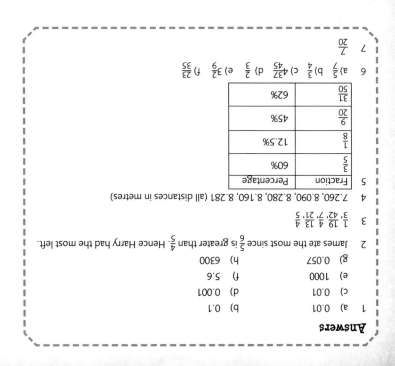

Making a point

You and three friends have won £1, which you want to divide into 4 equal parts. You receive £0.25. This ends with the digit '5' after 2 decimal places and is called a <u>terminating decimal</u>.

If, however, you had shared your winnings with two friends, you would have divided £1 into 3 equal parts and received £0.3333... each. The digit '3' is repeated for an infinite number of decimal places. This is called a <u>recurring decimal</u>.

In the examples above, fractions are 'changed' into decimals.

1 $\frac{1}{4}$ = 0.25 (No repeating digits.)

2 $\frac{1}{3}$ = 0.33333... As the digit '3' is repeated forever, or infinitely, the answer is written as $0.\dot{3}$ with a dot over the 3 to show it repeats.

3 If you turn the fraction $\frac{1}{11}$ into a decimal, it becomes 0.09090909... This is written as $0.\dot{0}\dot{9}$ with one dot over the '0' in the first decimal place and another over the '9' to show that they both repeat.

4 If you turn the the fraction $\frac{1}{13}$ into a decimal, it becomes 0.076923076923... This can be written as $0.\dot{0}7692\dot{3}$ with one dot over the '0' in the first decimal place and another over the '3'. This shows that all the digits '076923' repeat.

Sometimes it is useful to know quantities in percentages. The word 'percentage' is just another way of saying hundredths. You just multiply your fraction or decimal by 100.

1 Multiplying $\frac{1}{4}$ by 100 is the same as dividing 100 by 4. When 0.25 is multiplied by 100, the position of the decimal point moves 2 places to the right.

$$\frac{1}{4} \times 100 = \frac{100}{4} = 25\% \text{ or } 0.25 \times 100 = 25\%$$

2 Multiplying $\frac{1}{3}$ by 100 is the same as dividing 100 by 3. When 0.3 is multiplied by 100, the position of the decimal point moves 2 places to the right. As this is a recurring decimal, it is usual to give this percentage as a fraction.

$$\frac{1}{3} \times 100 = \frac{100}{3} = 33\frac{1}{3}\% \text{ or } 0.\dot{3} \times 100 = 33\frac{1}{3}\%$$

3 Multiplying $\frac{1}{11}$ by 100 is the same as dividing 100 by 11. When 0.09 is multiplied by 100, the position of the decimal point moves 2 places to the right. As this is a recurring decimal, it is usual to give this percentage as a fraction.

$$\frac{1}{11} \times 100 = \frac{100}{11} = 9\frac{1}{11}\% \text{ or } 0.\dot{0}\dot{9} \times 100 = 9\frac{1}{11}\%$$

4 Multiplying $\frac{1}{13}$ by 100 is the same as dividing 100 by 13. When 0.076923 is multiplied by 100, the position of the decimal point moves 2 places to the right. As this is a recurring decimal, it is usual to give this percentage as a fraction.

$$\frac{1}{13} \times 100 = \frac{100}{13} = 7\frac{9}{13}\% \text{ or } 0.\dot{0}7692\dot{3} \times 100 = 7\frac{9}{13}\%$$

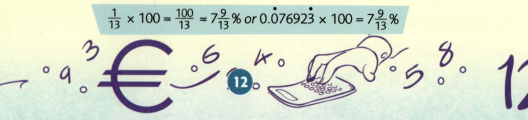

Match up

1 The measurements in the left-hand column need to be corrected to 2 decimal places. Draw a line from each measurement in the left-hand column to its corrected value in the right-hand column.

3.543 21 m	3.01
2.680 12 m	4.04
4.037 55 m	1.90
3.005 55 m	2.68
2.800 16 m	3.54
1.897 56 m	3.69
3.689 51 m	2.80

Fill the gaps

2 a) A bath measures 1.670 25 m by 0.736 54 m. These measurements corrected to 1 decimal place are .... m and .... m.

   b) The bathroom floor measures 3.543 21 m by 2.680 12 m. Its area is .... m^2 when the measurements are corrected to two decimal places.

   c) You should use corrected measurements because ....

   d) The percentage of the floor area covered by the bath is .... %.

   e) The percentage of the floor area that needs to be covered by flooring is .... %.

   f) .... is the area of flooring required given to an appropriate number of decimal places.

Profit or loss?

A house cost £135 000 when it was bought two years ago. The estate agent said it would <u>increase</u> in value each year at a rate of 5%.

What should its value be now?

There are two ways of working out the increased value.

1. Work out the actual increase and then add it to the original cost.

    First year increase = 5% of £135 000
    $= \frac{5}{100} \times 135\,000 = £6750$

    ∴ value at end of first year
    = £141 750.

    Second year increase = 5% of £141 750
    $= \frac{5}{100} \times 141\,750 = £7087.50$

    ∴ value at end of second year
    = £148 837.50.

2. After one year the value will be 105% (100% + 5%) of the original cost.

    ∴ value at end of first year = 105% of £135 000 $= \frac{105}{100} \times 135\,000 = £141\,750$

    and value at end of second year = 105% of £141 750 $= \frac{105}{100} \times 141\,750 = £148\,837.50$

Is this a <u>profit</u> or a <u>loss</u>?

The new value is greater than the original cost, so a profit has been made.

What is the difference in value?

The difference in value (profit) is found by subtracting the original cost from the increased value. Profit = £148 837.50 − £135 000 = £13 837.50

What percentage difference is this?

The percentage profit is found by dividing the profit by the original cost and multiplying the answer by 100.

$$\frac{13\,837.50}{135\,000} \times 100 = 10.25\%$$

What's the profit?

1 You are given some money for your birthday. In total, it comes to £50. You put it in a savings account. The interest rate is 4.85%. Complete the table to show its value, to two decimal places, in future years.

Number of years	Value
1 year	
2 years	
5 years	

2 The interest rate changes to 5.15% after the first year. £ .... will be in your account at the end of the second year.

3 The local stationery shop is offering two sets of coloured pencils for the price of one. You decide to keep one set and sell the other to raise money for the local charity. You pay £2.50 for the two sets and sell the second set for £1.50.

Tick the correct option in the following.

a) Do you make a profit or loss?   profit ☐   loss ☐

b) How much?   20p ☐   25p ☐   50p ☐

c) What percentage is this of the original cost?   20% ☐   25% ☐   50% ☐

4 The owners of a café grow their own vegetables, costing 50p per cabbage, after taking into account all their expenses. There are more cabbages than they can cope with in the kitchen. They decide to sell the surplus at 35p per cabbage.

a) Do they make a profit or loss on each surplus cabbage?   profit ☐   loss ☐

b) How much?   10p ☐   15p ☐   20p ☐

c) What percentage per cabbage?   20% ☐   25% ☐   30% ☐

KEY FACTS

⬆ If the original value is greater than the final value, a loss has been made.

➡ If the original value is less than the final value, a profit has been made.

⬇ To find the percentage profit or loss, use the formula

$$\frac{profit (loss)}{original\ value} \times 100$$

• TOP TIPS •

To find profit or loss, remember to compare final value with original value.

Fishy business

Your class has been asked to cook lunch for some special guests. There will be ten people at the lunch.

Here is a recipe for fish pie, which serves six people.

450 g white fish fillets
1.2 litres milk
450 g potatoes
450 g tomatoes
300 g mushrooms
240 g frozen peas
57 g grated cheese

You can work out the quantities of these ingredients in the proportions needed to serve ten people by using the unitary method.

1 Work out the quantity of each ingredient for one person. You need to divide each quantity by 6. (The ingredients are measured in grams, so do not need to be converted.)

Here is the recipe for one person.

75 g white fish fillets
0.2 litres milk
75 g potatoes
75 g tomatoes
50 g mushrooms
40 g frozen peas
9.5 g grated cheese

2 Multiply each quantity by 10 to obtain amount required for ten people.

Here is the recipe for ten people.

750 g white fish fillets
2 litres milk
750 g potatoes
750 g tomatoes
500 g mushrooms
400 g frozen peas
95 g grated cheese

What is the <u>ratio</u> of fish to mushrooms to peas to cheese in the original recipe?

1 The ratio of fish to mushrooms to peas to cheese is written as
fish : mushrooms : peas : cheese = 450 : 300 : 240 : 57

2 The ratio is not in its lowest terms, as the numbers have a common factor of 3.

3 Divide each number by 3, giving the ratio fish : mushrooms : peas : cheese = 150 : 100 : 80 : 19

12

Crack the codes

1 A cook has three different recipes for sauce.
Fill in the gaps with the ratio of ingredients for each sauce.

(i) thick sauce: 42 g flour, 42 g butter, 420 ml liquid

1	:		:	**10**

(ii) medium sauce: 42 g flour, 42 g butter, 490 ml liquid

	:		:	**35**

(iii) thin sauce: 42 g flour, 42 g butter, 560 ml liquid

3	:		:	

2 Are these ratios in their lowest terms? If yes, colour the square for the ratio in the grid below **red**. If no, colour the square for the ratio in the grid below **blue**.

(i) 125 g : 250 g
(ii) 53 ml : 35 ml
(iii) 225 ml : 450 ml : 300 ml
(iv) 1 l : 500 ml : 0.25 l
(v) 123 g : 323 g
(vi) 0.75 kg : 300 g : 1.5 kg

(i)	(ii)	(iii)
(iv)	(v)	(vi)

Which pattern have you made?

A

B

C

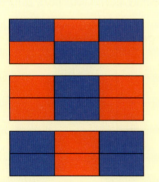

If your answer for any of the ratios above was no, convert them into their lowest terms. ....

3 Four friends buy a packet of biscuits for £1.98. They split the cost between them and divide the 44 biscuits accordingly. Izzy paid 36p, Nikki paid 45p, Dan paid 63p and Jem paid 54p. Join the names to the number of biscuits they received from the packet.

Name	Number of biscuits
Izzy	14
Nikki	10
Dan	12
Jem	8

Test your knowledge 2

1 Write the following fractions as decimals.

a) $\frac{1}{6}$ =   b) $\frac{4}{5}$ =

c) $\frac{1}{3}$ =   d) $\frac{2}{11}$ =

e) $\frac{2}{5}$ =

(5 marks)

2 The table shows some decimals. Round each of the decimals to the nearest whole number, one decimal place and two decimal places.

Decimal	Nearest whole number	One decimal place	Two decimal places
6.439			
27.372			
15.625			

(9 marks)

3 The table below shows some equivalent decimals and percentages. Complete the table.

Decimal	Percentage
0.65	
0.273	
	24%
	37%

(4 marks)

4 a) Increase £60 by 15%   **(2 marks)**

    b) Decrease £130 by 30%   **(2 marks)**

5 Samuel bought a computer for £899. He sold it two years later and made a 35% loss. What price did he sell it for?

(2 marks)

6 A football stadium seats 4800 people. Another stand has been built so that the total number of seats has increased by 12%. How many people can the stadium seat now?

(2 marks)

7 A recipe uses 1.4 kg of flour and 500 g of sugar. Write in its simplest form the ratio of flour to sugar.

(2 marks)

8 A nut mix has cashews, almonds and peanuts in the ratio 1 : 3 : 5. How many grams of cashews and almonds are needed to mix with 250 g of peanuts?

(2 marks)

9 Robert, Daisy and Charlotte share the cost of a meal in the ratio 2 : 6 : 3. The meal costs £77. How much should each pay?

(2 marks)

(Total 32 marks)

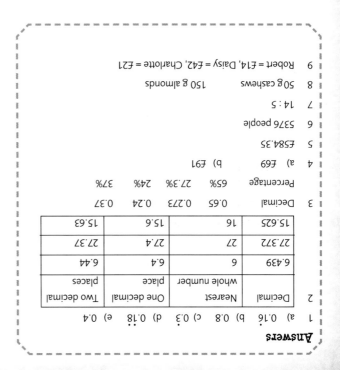

Answers

1 a) 0.16 b) 0.8 c) $0.\dot{3}$ d) $0.1\dot{8}$ e) 0.4

2

Decimal	Nearest whole number	One decimal place	Two decimal places
15.625	16	15.6	15.63
27.372	27	27.4	27.37
6.439	6	6.4	6.44

3

Decimal	0.65	0.273	0.24	0.37
Percentage	65%	27.3%	24%	37%

4 a) £69 b) £91

5 £584.35

6 5376 people

7 14 : 5

8 50 g cashews   150 g almonds

9 Robert = £14, Daisy = £42, Charlotte = £21

Up and down

Numbers with a sign in front of them are known as <u>directed numbers</u>, as the sign gives the direction taken using a number line.

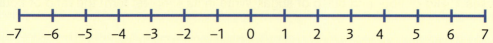

You can check the weather in different towns around the world on various websites. On one particular February day, the temperatures are as follows:

Brisbane	27°C
Chicago	−7°C
Hong Kong	17°C
Johannesburg	14°C
Moscow	−14°C
New York	−4°C
Paris	1°C
Vancouver	7°C
Zurich	−2°C

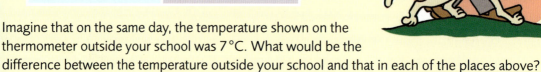

Imagine that on the same day, the temperature shown on the thermometer outside your school was 7°C. What would be the difference between the temperature outside your school and that in each of the places above?

Place	Temperature	Calculation	Difference (number of degrees)
Brisbane	27°C	27°C − 7°C	20
Chicago	−7°C	7°C − (−7°C)	14
Hong Kong	17°C	17°C − 7°C	10
Johannesburg	14°C	14°C − 7°C	7
Moscow	−14°C	7°C − (−14°C)	21
New York	−4°C	7°C − (−4°C)	11
Paris	1°C	7°C − 1°C	6
Vancouver	7°C	7°C − 7°C	0
Zurich	−2°C	7°C − (−2°C)	9

In the calculations, −(−7) is the same as +7. If there is no sign, assume the number is positive as in +7. If there is a minus sign, the number is a <u>negative number</u> as in −7.

Match up

1 Your headteacher goes to a local hotel for a meeting. She parks her car in the underground car park (CP), walks up the stairs and enters the building at ground floor level (G). The cloakroom is in the basement (−1), morning coffee is served two floors up and the meeting room is three floors above that.

Connect the correct lift button to each destination.

2 The total number of floors your headteacher passes to collect her coat and car before she leaves the hotel is ___.

3 Adam wants to go on a diving holiday to look at wrecks. He finds a website giving details about the dives in this diagram.

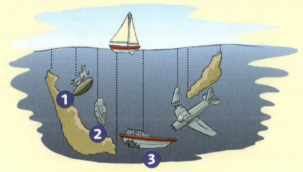

Draw lines and write these distances on the diagram.

a) What is the distance needed to dive from the boat to the shipwreck 1?

b) How far above shipwreck 3 is the side of the boat?

c) How far below the tip of the mast is the bottom of each reef?

d) What is the distance between shipwreck 2 and the aeroplane?

cloakroom

coffee

G

meeting room

CP

Happy birthday!

Six members of the Aswani family have birthdays in the same month, on the 18th, 19th, 20th, 23rd, 25th and 27th. Is there a connection between these numbers? If so, what is it?

First check the <u>factors</u> and <u>prime</u> factors of each number.

Number	Factors	Prime factors
18	1, 2, 3, 6, 9, 18	$2 \times 3 \times 3 = 2 \times 3^2$
19	1, 19	1×19
20	1, 2, 4, 5, 10, 20	$2 \times 2 \times 5 = 2^2 \times 5$
25	1, 5, 25	$5 \times 5 = 5^2$
27	1, 3, 9, 27	$3 \times 3 \times 3 = 3^3$
28	1, 2, 4, 7, 14, 28	$2 \times 2 \times 7 = 2^2 \times 7$

From the table, we can see the following.

1 The numbers 18, 20 and 28 all have the factor 2, so they are <u>even</u> numbers. The rest are <u>odd</u> numbers.

2 The numbers 25 and 27 are special. 25 is a <u>square number</u> (it is 5 raised to the <u>power</u> 2 (5^2)) and 27 is a cube number (it is 3 raised to the power 3 (3^3)). The small digit indicating the power is called the <u>index</u>. It tells you how many times the number is written down and multiplied. For example, $7^4 = 7 \times 7 \times 7 \times 7 = 2401$. The inverse of raising a number to a power is finding the <u>root</u>. The square root of 25 ($\sqrt{25}$) is 5 and the cube root of 27 ($\sqrt[3]{27}$) is 3.

3 The number 19 is a prime number as it has only two factors, itself and 1.

4 Many of the numbers, such as 18 and 27, have common factors. The factors of 18 are 1, 2, 3, 6, 9 and 18 and the factors of 27 are 1, 3, 9 and 27.

- To find the <u>highest common factor</u> (HCF), write the numbers in their prime factors and extract their common factors.

  To find the HCF of 18 and 27, look at $18 = 2 \times 3^2$ and $27 = 3^3$. Both numbers include 3^2 ($3^3 = 3 \times 3^2$), so the HCF $= 3^2 = 9$.

  This means that 18 and 27 are <u>multiples</u> of 9. Other multiples of 9 are 36, 45, 54 and so on. (These numbers are in the 9 times table, but there are many more multiples of 9 beyond the table, such as $153 = 17 \times 9$.)

- To find the lowest common multiple (LCM), write the numbers in their prime factors and compare. To find the LCM of 18 and 20, compare $18 = 2 \times 3^2$ and $20 = 2^2 \times 5$.

  Any multiple of 18 must be 2×3^2 and any multiple of 20 must include $2^2 \times 5$, so the LCM of 18 and 20 must be $2^2 \times 5 \times 3^2 = 180$.

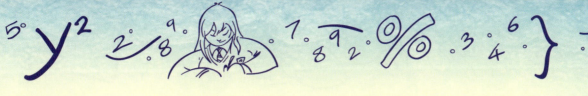

Puzzles

Here are some puzzles about prime numbers, powers and roots.

1 Colour all prime numbers yellow. How many are there between 1 and 100? ....

1	2	3	4	5	6	7	8	9	10
11	12	13	14	15	16	17	18	19	20
21	22	23	24	25	26	27	28	29	30
31	32	33	34	35	36	37	38	39	40
41	42	43	44	45	46	47	48	49	50
51	52	53	54	55	56	57	58	59	60
61	62	63	64	65	66	67	68	69	70
71	72	73	74	75	76	77	78	79	80
81	82	83	84	85	86	87	88	89	90
91	92	93	94	95	96	97	98	99	100

· TOP TIPS ·

1 Any number raised to the power zero equals 1.

2 Change numbers into the product of their prime factors before finding their LCM and HCF.

2 a) Put a green cross on multiples of 5.
   b) Find the square roots of the multiples of 5 up to and including 30. ....

3 Put a red line through the HCFs (highest common factors) of:

   a) 30 and 54
   b) 20, 28 and 36

4 Put a blue line through the LCMs (lowest common multiples) of:

   a) 8 and 12
   b) 5, 9 and 15

5 Write your answers to these questions in the grid below. Put decimal points in their own square.

   a) 3^2
   b) 5^2
   c) 2.3^2
   d) 4.1^2
   e) 2^3
   f) 3.5^3

KEY FACTS

↑ A factor is a number that divides into another exactly, without a remainder.

→ A prime number has only two factors, itself and 1.

↓ An even number always has a factor 2.

↑ A number has the factor 3 if the sum of its digits is divisible by 3.

← A number has the factor 5 if it ends in 5 or 0.

→ The HCF of one or more numbers is the highest factor common to those numbers.

↑ The LCM of one or more numbers is the lowest multiple common to those numbers.

↓ A multiple of a number can be divided exactly by that number, without a remainder.

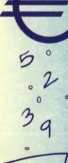

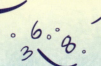

Which key?

You have a new calculator and use the instruction booklet to learn how to use the keys. You and a friend have a competition to see how quickly you can work out the same problem.

$$\frac{62.3 \times 8.55}{8.25 - (5.34 - 2.49)}$$

You get an answer of 98.64166667 and your friend gets 61.71545455.

Which is correct?

You key in the bottom of the calculation (8.25 − (5.34 − 2.49)) and store it in the calculator memory. (Use STO, Min or M+ depending on your calculator.) You then key in the top of the calculation (62.3 × 8.55), followed by ÷. You then recall the stored memory. (This may be RCL then M, RM or MR. Check your instruction book, as there are many different types of calculator keypads.) The final key is =. Your answer is 98.64166667.

If unlimited decimal places were displayed, the answer would show the recurring decimal 98.6416666... The calculator has corrected this to eight decimal places, giving a final digit of 7.

You check it by keying in 62.3 × 8.55 ÷ (8.25 − (5.34 − 2.49)) =. This gives the same result, so it must be correct.

What mistakes were made by the other person?

Your friend keys in 62.3 × 8.55 ÷ 8.25 − (5.34 − 2.49) =. This gives the answer 61.71545455, again a recurring decimal corrected to 8 decimal places. This is incorrect. The calculator thinks that it has calculated $62.3 \times \frac{8.55}{8.25}$ then subtracted (5.34 − 2.49).

How could the mistakes be avoided?

The mistakes can be avoided by using <u>estimation</u> to find the answer to the correct order of magnitude. Each number is rounded to the nearest whole number. As the first stage is an <u>approximation</u>, ≈ is used. When the rounding has been done, = can be used as the following stages are exact.

$$\frac{62.3 \times 8.55}{8.25 - (5.34 - 2.49)} \approx \frac{60 \times 9}{8 - (5 - 2)} = \frac{540}{5} = 108$$

Your answer is obviously more sensible than your friend's result.

The Key Facts section on the next page gives some guidance on the use of other calculator keys.

Match up

1 You are given three answers to each of these questions. Draw a red line to an accurate answer, a blue line to an estimation and a green line to an answer that is corrected to 2 decimal places.

$\dfrac{6.37 - 3.26}{6.37 + 3.26}$	0.39 0.32 0.322949117
$5 \times (6.78)^2$	229.842 245 229.84
$3 \div \sqrt{53.29}$	0.41 $\dfrac{3}{7}$ 0.410958904
$(3.55 \times 1.24) + (8.32 \div 4.1)$	6.431268293 6.43 6

• TOP TIPS •

1 Use your calculator's instruction book to learn how your calculator works.

2 Always enter numbers in the correct order. Remembering BODMAS helps (see Key Facts).

3 Ask yourself if your answer is sensible.

2 Use your calculator fraction and percentage keys to find which of these are the answers to the questions below.

$$1\frac{13}{24} \qquad 4\frac{1}{9} \qquad 70\% \qquad 1\frac{1}{8} \qquad 55.5\% \qquad \frac{23}{4}$$

(i) $\dfrac{3}{8} + \dfrac{3}{4}$ (ii) $2\dfrac{7}{8} - 1\dfrac{1}{3}$ (iii) $5\dfrac{3}{4}$ as an improper fraction (iv) $\dfrac{37}{9}$ as a mixed number

(v) $\dfrac{56}{80}$ as a percentage (vi) $\dfrac{35}{63}$ as a percentage

KEY FACTS

⬆ Use estimation to give you an idea of the order of magnitude for the answer.

➡ **BODMAS** gives you the correct order of operation of your calculation.

Brackets, **O**rders or powers, **D**ivision & **M**ultiplication, **A**ddition & **S**ubtraction

(You will sometimes see BIDMAS, where I represents Indices.)

⬇ Using the 'bracket' keys means that you can separate parts of a calculation.

⬆ Use the Memory function to store and recall different parts of a calculation.

⬆ A sign change key (+ / –) changes the signs of numbers.

⬅ Fractions can be entered using the fraction key ab/c, where 'a' is the whole number, 'b' is the numerator and 'c' is the denominator. A mixed number can be changed to an improper fraction using the $\frac{d}{c}$ key. For example, $6\frac{3}{8} \rightarrow 6\rfloor3\rfloor8$ shift $\frac{d}{c} \rightarrow 51\rfloor8$. Conversely, an improper fraction entered using the $a\frac{b}{c}$ key, followed by = will give the display $6\rfloor3\rfloor8$, which is the mixed number $6\frac{3}{8}$.

➡ Percentages can be calculated using the % key. You may need to use the shift key to access %. ($\frac{27}{45}$ as % $\rightarrow 27 \div 45\% \rightarrow 60\%$)

⬇ Powers may be entered using the x^2, x^3 or x^y key and roots using $\sqrt{\,}$, $\sqrt[3]{\,}$ or $\sqrt[x]{\,}$ keys.

Test your knowledge 3

1   Without using a calculator work out the following.

    a) 426 × 25 ....   b) 2.15 × 25 ....

    c) 32 × 5 ....   d) 18 × 8 ....

    e) 6275 ÷ 25 ....   f) 1025 ÷ 25 ....

(6 marks)

2   Without using a calculator work out the answers to the following.

    a) −2 + 7 ....   b) −6 − 3 ....

    c) −2 × 9 ....   d) −25 ÷ −5 ....

    e) −4 × −3 ....   f) −6 − 10 + 8 ....

(6 marks)

3   On this pyramid, each pair of numbers is added to get the number above. Fill in the missing numbers.

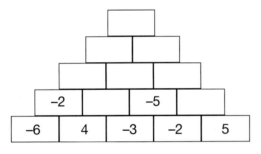

(8 marks)

4   Fill in the missing numbers in the following statements.

    a) 4 cubed equals ....

    b) 1000 is the cube of ....

    c) The cube root of 27 is ....

    d) The cube root of 125 is ....

    e) .... is the cube root of 1

(5 marks)

5 Find the square root of the following, without using a calculator.

a) 64

b) 196

c) 49

(3 marks)

6 Write down each of these numbers as a product of prime factors.

a) 32

b) 60

(2 marks)

7 Use a calculator to work out the following. Give your answer to 2 decimal places.

a) $5 \times (2.71)^2$

b) $\sqrt[3]{70}$

c) $7 \times (3.16)^3$

d) $\sqrt{28} \times (1.2)^2$

(4 marks)

(Total 34 marks)

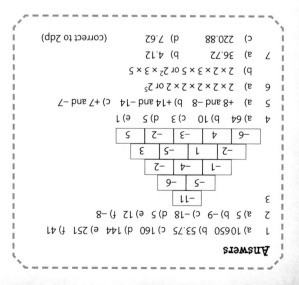

On the track

Your local music store sells CDs, videos and DVDs. The owners would like to have some idea of the proportion of sales of the different items. They decide to look at the quantity of each item sold in one day.

They worked out that usually there were three times as many CDs sold as DVDs and twice as many DVDs as videos.

1 Write an algebraic expression for the quantities of CDs and DVDs sold in terms of videos.

An <u>algebraic expression</u> is a statement using symbols instead of words.

Choose a letter to represent the variable quantity of each item, so let the number of CDs be c, DVDs be d and videos be v.

An expression for the quantities of DVDs sold in terms of videos, i.e. twice as many DVDs as videos, becomes $2v$.

An expression for the quantities of CDs sold in terms of videos, i.e. three times as many CDs as DVDs, becomes $3 \times 2v = 6v$.

2 Write an expression for the quantities of DVDs and videos sold in terms of CDs.

- If three times as many CDs as DVDs are sold, then a third as many DVDs as CDs are sold. An expression for the quantities of DVDs sold in terms of CDs becomes $c/3$.

- If twice as many DVDs as videos are sold, then half as many videos as DVDs are sold. An expression for the quantities of videos sold in terms of CDs becomes $\frac{1}{2}(c/3) = c/6$.

- They actually sold the following quantities over an August weekend.

> Saturday: 24 CDs, 13 DVDs and 9 videos
>
> Sunday: 16 CDs, 7 DVDs and 6 videos

3 Write an expression for the items sold over each day and over the whole weekend.

- Using the same letters for the items, Saturday's sales of 24 CDs, 13 DVDs and 9 videos becomes $24c + 13d + 9v$

- Sunday's sales of 16 CDs, 7 DVDs and 6 videos becomes $16c + 7d + 6v$

- The whole weekend sales become $24c + 13d + 9v + 16c + 7d + 6v$

4 Simplify your expression by <u>collecting like terms</u>.

Collect together the c terms, d terms and v terms:

$24c + 13d + 9v + 16c + 7d + 6v \rightarrow 40c + 20d + 15v$

Match up

1 Match up the expressions for lunchtime sales each day, using c (CD), d (DVD) and v (video), with the sales.

Monday: four CDs, three DVDs, two videos	$5c + 2d + 2v$
Tuesday: three CDs, two DVDs, four videos	$20c + 14d + 13v$
Wednesday: two CDs, two DVDs, one video	$3c + 2d + 4v$
Thursday: five CDs, two DVDs, two videos	$6c + 5d + 4v$
Friday: six CDs, five DVDs, four videos	$4c + 3d + 2v$
Total (Mon–Fri): .... CDs, ... DVDs, ... videos	$2c + 2d + v$

2 In a <u>magic square</u> the columns, rows and diagonals have the same sum. Is this a magic square? Show all your working.

$a - b$	$a + b - c$	$a + c$
$a + b + c$	a	$a - b - c$
$a - c$	$a - b + c$	$a + b$

KEY FACTS

↑ $3 \times a$ is $3a$ and $b \div 2$ is $b/2$

→ Collecting like terms means gathering together terms involving the same letters with the same powers, e.g. $a^2 + 2a^2 = 3a^2$, but $a^2 - 3b^2 + a^3$ cannot be simplified.

↓ It is not necessary to write $1a$, just write a.

Translating letters

Julia does a newspaper round in the village. She earns a basic wage of £2 plus 10p for delivering a weekday paper, 15p for a Saturday paper and 20p for a Sunday paper. Every house has a paper delivered every day.

Here are 4 steps to show you how to write a <u>formula</u> for the girl's earnings.

1 **Choose letters to represent the things that change**. These are known as <u>variables</u>. In this example, you could use h to represent each house receiving a paper and E to represent the girl's weekly wage.

2 **Find the girl's delivery earnings**. On weekdays these are 10p × h (this is the same as 10hp), on Saturdays these are 15p × h (this is the same as 15hp) and on Sundays these are 20p × h (this is the same as 20hp).

Add these together to find her total delivery earnings. These are: (10h + 15h + 20h)p.
Simplify this by collecting these like terms → 45h pence.

3 **Add her basic wage of £2 to her delivery earnings**. These are: £2 (This is known as a constant term as it does not change.) Her total earnings are £2 + 45h pence.

4 **Make the units of all terms the same by changing pounds to pence**.
£2 to 200 pence → 200 + 45h

The formula becomes 200 + 45h = E

You can use the formula to work out how many houses have a paper delivery, if Julia earns a total of £20.

Her wage is £20, so <u>substitute</u> 2000 (£20 in pence) for E.

$$200 + 45h = 2000$$
$$45h = 2000 - 200$$
$$45h = 1800$$
$$h = 1800 \div 45$$
$$\therefore h = 40$$

Julia delivers to 40 houses.

How much would she earn if there were 35 houses receiving a daily paper?

Julia delivers to 35 houses, so substitute 35 for h. It is a good idea to use brackets to make the order of calculation clear.

$$200 + (45 \times 35) = E$$
$$200 + 1575 = E$$
$$1775 = E \text{ (in pence)}$$
Divide this by 100 to convert to £.
Julia's weekly wage is £17.75

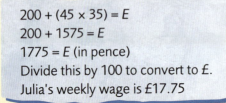

Fill the gaps

Some thermometers show the temperature in the Fahrenheit scale and others in the Celsius scale.

1 To convert from Fahrenheit to Celsius, you need to subtract 32, multiply the result by 5 and then divide by 9. Fill the gaps to complete the formula to convert Fahrenheit scale to Celsius scale.

$$°C = ...(°F - ...)/...$$

2 To convert from Celsius to Fahrenheit, multiply by 9, divide by 5 and add 32.

$$°F = ...°C/... + ...$$

3 Match the temperatures on these 2 thermometers.

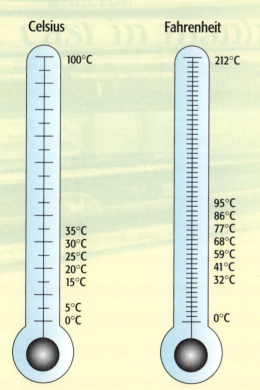

Celsius

100°C

35°C
30°C
25°C
20°C
15°C

5°C
0°C

Fahrenheit

212°C

95°C
86°C
77°C
68°C
59°C
41°C
32°C

0°C

What is it?

Your new puppy needs a fenced piece of lawn in which to play, so you make a play area in the shape of a rectangle, as below.

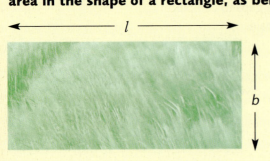

Here's how to write an <u>equation</u>, using l and b, for finding the <u>perimeter</u> of the play area. P is used to represent the perimeter, the distance round the rectangle:

$$P = l + b + l + b$$

$$P = 2l + 2b \text{ or } P = 2(l + b)$$

Say you're told that the length is 4.5 metres and the breadth is 2.75 metres. How can you use your equation to find the perimeter?

You substitute these values into your equation for the perimeter.

$$P = 2(4.5 + 2.75) = 2(7.25). \text{ This is the same as } 2 \times 7.25.$$

$$P = 14.50$$

$$\therefore \text{ The perimeter is 14.5 metres.}$$

Here's how to write an equation, using l and b, for finding the <u>area</u> of the play area.

The area of a rectangle is the product of the length and the breadth. A is used to represent the area of the rectangle:

$$A = l \times b \text{ or } A = lb$$

If the area required is 7 square metres and the breadth is 2 metres, use your equation to find the length.

You are told that $A = 7$ square metres and $b = 2$ metres. Substitute these values into your equation for the area.

$$7 = l \times 2$$

This means that $l = 7 \div 2 = 3.5$

The length is 3.5 metres.

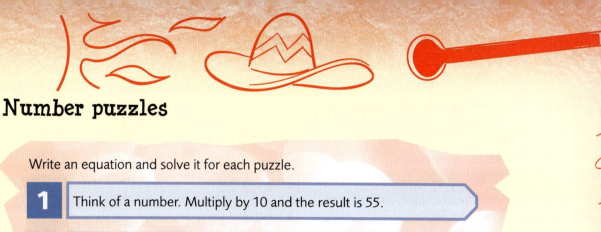

Number puzzles

Write an equation and solve it for each puzzle.

1 Think of a number. Multiply by 10 and the result is 55.

2 Think of a number. Double it and add 5. The answer is the same as if you add 7 to the original number.

3 Adam is three years older than Ben, who is twice Callum's age. If you add their three ages, the answer is 33. Find the age of each of them.

4 The angles in a triangle are x, y and z. Angle y is twice angle x. Angle z is three times angle x. Find the three angles.

5 The angles in a quadrilateral are p, q, r and s. Angle q is twice angle p. Angle r is twice angle q and angle s is the sum of angle p and angle r. Find all four angles.

6 In a class of 28 pupils, there are three times as many pupils with brown eyes as there are with blue eyes. How many pupils are there with each eye colour?

KEY FACTS

↑ When you are writing an equation, try to remember that facts from all sections of maths apply, e.g. how to work out area.

⇥ You will be solving your equation to find an unknown variable. Give this variable a letter and explain what it means.

• TOP TIPS •

1 Maths is a language, so remember to translate from words to symbols

2 Remember that an equation needs an equals sign (=).

Test your knowledge 4

1 Simplify these expressions.

    a) $2 \times 3y$

    b) $4 \times b \times b$

    c) $(a + b) \div c$

    d) $a \times (b + d)$

                                              (4 marks)

2 Simplify these expressions.

    a) $2a + a + a$

    b) $3a - 2a + 4a$

    c) $5a + 2b + 3a + 4b$

    d) $5m - 3n + 6n - n$

    e) $3n + 5 - 2n - 6$

    f) $3a^2 - 2a^2 + 6a$

                                              (6 marks)

3 Multiply out the brackets:

    a) $4 (x + 2)$

    b) $3 (x - 4)$

    c) $a (a + b)$

    d) $5 - (n - 2)$

                                              (4 marks)

4 Find the values of these expressions when $a = 2$.

    a) $5a - 3$

    b) $2a^2 + 1$

    c) $3a^3$

                                              (3 marks)

5 Find the value of y when $x = -4$.

    a) $y = \dfrac{2x + 3}{x}$

    b) $y = \dfrac{4 + 2x}{x + 1}$

                                              (2 marks)

6 The formula for the perimeter P of a rectangle with dimensions l and w is

    $P = 2(l + w)$

    If $P = 40$ and $l = 14$, what is w?

                                              (2 marks)

7 Solve these equations.

   a) $n - 6 = 4$

   c) $3a + 2 = 11$

   e) $\dfrac{2x}{3} = 4$

   b) $2a = 12$

   d) $5m - 6 = 19$

   f) $3(n + 2) = 9$

(6 marks)

8 Solve these equations.

   a) $5n + 2 = 3n + 6$

   c) $4m - 3 = 2m + 6$

   b) $5y - 2 = 2y + 7$

   d) $2(b - 1) + 3(b + 1) = 21$

(4 marks)

(Total 31 marks)

Which pattern?

A tiler has been asked to tile a bathroom. He wants to design a pattern with coloured tiles. He looks at the following possibilities.

a) □□, □□, □□□, □□□□, ...
   □□ □□□ □□□□ , ...

b) □□, □□, □□□□, □□□□□□□□ , ...
   □□ □□□□ □□□□□□□□ , ...

These are <u>number patterns</u> or <u>sequences</u>. Each item (tile) in the pattern is called a <u>term</u>. The general rule for a number pattern is also known as the nth term and is useful for predicting terms later in the sequence.

To find the rule ask yourself these questions.

1 Is the same number added or subtracted to find the next term? This is called the common difference.

2 Is the same number multiplying or dividing to find the next term? This is called a constant factor.

3 Are the terms special numbers, such as primes, squares, cubes, triangular numbers or powers of the same number?

Find the general rule for each of the tiler's choices.

Use it to see how many tiles he needs for the 10th pattern.

The number of tiles in pattern a are 2, 4, 6, 8,... There is a common difference of 2. Call the first term T_1, the second T_2, and so on.

$T_1 = 2 = (2 \times 1)$, $T_2 = 4 = (2 \times 2)$, $T_3 = 6 = (2 \times 3)$, $T_4 = 8 = (2 \times 4)$, so $T_n = 2 \times n$ or $2n$

$\therefore T_{10} = 2 \times 10 = 20$

The number of tiles in pattern b are 2, 4, 8, 16,... There is a constant factor of 2.

$T_1 = 2$, $T_2 = 4 = (2 \times 2)$, $T_3 = 8 = (2 \times 2 \times 2)$, $T_4 = 16 = (2 \times 2 \times 2 \times 2)$ so $T_n = 2^n$

$\therefore T_{10} = 2^{10} = 1024$

Fill the gaps

1 You are given a pair of rabbits in January. After two months, they produce another pair of rabbits and continue to produce a new pair every month after that. Each new pair of rabbits produces another new pair after two months and then produces a new pair each month. Complete the table below. How many pairs of rabbits will you have in December? .... pairs

Month	Jan	Feb	Mar	Apr	May	Jun	Jul	Aug	Sep	Oct	Nov	Dec
Number of rabbits	2	2	4			16			68			

2 These are some patterns made with matchsticks.

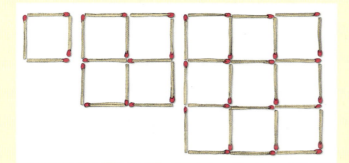

a) Complete the table below.

Term	1	2	3	4	5	6	7	8	9	10
Squares	1	4	9		25			64		
Matchsticks	4	12	24			84		180		

b) The number of squares is given by the .... of the term.

c) To find a general rule for the number of matchsticks, find the .... between the terms. The second .... is a constant number, ...

3 In a Year 8 class, pupils sit round tables.

a) Complete the table below.

Number of tables	1	2	3	4
Number of pupils	4		8	

b) The number of pupils is found by .... to each term

c) If the tables are grouped in threes, ... tables are needed for a class of 24.

TOP TIPS

It is useful to remember the common number patterns, such as squares, cubes, triangular numbers and common multiples.

KEY FACTS

↑ Look for a common difference between terms (where terms are either added or subtracted to generate further terms).

→ Look for a constant factor (where terms are either multiplied or divided to generate further terms).

↓ Once a pattern has been found, translate this into a general rule for the *n*th term. This means you can find any term by substituting the term into the rule.

On the straight

Suppose that your maths homework is to draw the <u>graph</u> $y = x$. You would start by working out your table of <u>coordinates</u> and plot the points on graph paper (squared paper).

x	−2	−1	0	1	2
y	−2	−1	0	1	2

Next you decide to see what will happen if you have these equations.

   a $y = 2x$
   b $y = 3x$
   c $y = -2x$
   d $y = 2x + 1$

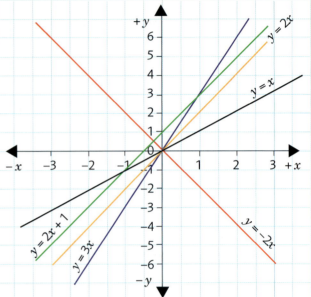

You need to produce a table of coordinates for each of the linear functions. (These are equations that produce a straight-line graph.) The general equation for a straight-line graph is $y = mx + c$. The <u>gradient</u> or slope of the line is m, the coefficient of x. The line crosses, or intercepts, the y-axis at the point $(0, c)$. The value of c is called the y-<u>intercept</u>.

As you are drawing all the lines on the same axes, it is convenient to use the same x-values in each case. Substitute these x-values in the equations to find the y-values.

a $y = 2x$

x	−2	−1	0	1	2
y	−4	−2	0	2	4

b $y = 3x$

x	−2	−1	0	1	2
y	−6	−3	0	3	6

c $y = -2x$

x	−2	−1	0	1	2
y	4	2	0	−2	−4

d $y = 2x + 1$

x	−2	−1	0	1	2
y	−3	−1	1	3	5

Lines **a** and **b** pass through the origin like $y = x$ but are steeper. The gradient of $y = x$ is 1, $y = 2x$ has a gradient of 2 and the gradient of $y = 3x$ is 3. Line **c** also passes through the origin like $y = x$ but in the opposite direction, because the gradient of $y = -2x$ is −2. Line **d** cuts the y-axis at (0,1) and is parallel to line **a** as both lines have the same gradient of 2.

Match up

1 Match each table of coordinates with the correct equation.

$y = 4x$

a)

x	0	1	2	3	4
y	4	3	2	1	0

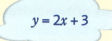
$y = 2x + 3$

$x + y = 4$

b)

x	−2	−1	0	1	2
y	−8	−4	0	4	8

$y = -x$

c)

x	−2	−1	0	1	2
y	2	1	0	−1	−2

d)

x	−2	−1	0	1	2
y	−1	1	3	5	7

2 All the pairs of coordinates in question 1 have been plotted in this diagram.

- Use a different colour to draw a straight line connecting a set of five points for each table.

- Write the equation on each line.

- Some points occur on more than one line.

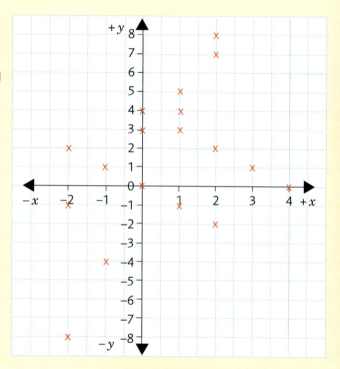

KEY FACTS

↑ **The equation of the x-axis is $y = 0$,** because y is always zero on the x-axis.

→ **The equation of the y-axis is $x = 0$,** because x is always zero on the y-axis.

↓ **The gradient of a line is the distance along (right or left) divided by the distance up or down. If the distance is right or up, it is positive. If the distance is left or down, it is negative.**

↑ **The general equation of a straight line is $y = mx + c$. The coefficient of x (number or letter multiplying x) is m and is the gradient of the line. The value c tells you where the line crosses the y-axis. This is known as the y-intercept.**

• TOP TIPS •

1 When giving coordinates, always write them in the form (x, y).

2 Before you draw a graph, work out your table of coordinates.

3 Use a sharp pencil to plot your coordinates accurately. Do not use ink because you cannot erase it without making a mess!

What's the plot?

Imagine you decide to buy some books from a company on the Internet. You compare the delivery charges of two different companies. The first company's delivery charges are shown in this table:

Number of books	Delivery charge
1	£2.50
2	£4.50
3	£6.50
4+	£7

The second company charges delivery of £1 per book ordered.

Below is a graph showing delivery charges for each company. The horizontal axis shows the number of books and the vertical axis shows delivery cost.

For the first company there is a short straight line up to 3 books, a less steep line between 3 and 4, followed by a horizontal line at £7 from 4 books onwards.

For the second company the points (1, £1), (2, £2), (3, £3) etc. have been joined to form a straight line.

a)   If you buy more than one book how much does the delivery charge of the first company increase?

You can calculate extra delivery charges from the table. From 1 to 3 books, you pay £2 extra each time. From 3 to 4 books, the difference is just 50p. For 4 books or more, there is a constant delivery charge of £7.

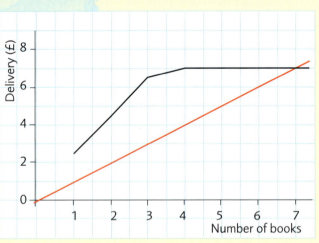

b)   Which company gives the best value (or best buy) in terms of delivery charge for

(i)   1 book   (ii) 5 books   (iii) 10 books?

It is easier to compare if a table is drawn.

Number of books	Delivery charges		Best value (or best buy)
	First company	Second company	
1	£2.50	£1	Second
5	£7	£5	Second
10	£7	£10	First

Fill the gaps

1 You have just received your mobile phone bill.

Number of minutes	0	20	40	60
Cost including fixed charge	£15	£17	£19	£21

a) The fixed charge is £ ....

b) You are being charged .... p per minute.

c) The total cost for 100 minutes is £ ....

d) The estimated number of minutes used when charged £22.50 is .... minutes.

2 You use a running machine to keep fit. You started a run at 0930 one morning.

This <u>distance–time graph</u> illustrates what happened.

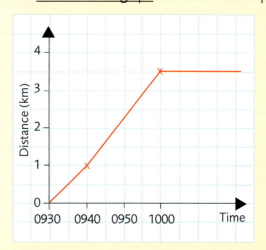

a) Your speed was .... km/h between 0930 and 0940.

b) You .... your speed at 0940.

c) You ran for .... minutes at this speed.

d) At 1000 you ....

· TOP TIPS ·

In a distance–time graph, time continues to the right. A return journey cannot go backwards in time.

KEY FACTS

↑ The gradient of a line gives the rate of change. In a distance–time graph the gradient gives the speed, so the steeper the line the greater the speed.

→ Fixed charges give the starting points on the vertical axis.

↓ Two journeys may be shown on the same axes. When vehicles pass one another, the lines cross.

Test your knowledge 5

1 Predict the next three terms of these sequences.

   a) 1, 3, 5, 7, ... , ... , ...

   b) 6, 12, 18, ... , ... , ...

   c) 1, 3, 6, 10, ... , ... , ...

   d) 1, 4, 9, 16, ... , ... , ...

   (12 marks)

2 The nth term of a sequence is given. Write the first five terms for each.

   a) $T_n = 2n + 1$

   b) $T_n = 3n - 2$

   c) $T_n = 10 - n$

   (3 marks)

3 Write down the nth term of these sequences.

   a) 2, 4, 6, 8, 10, ...

   b) 7, 10, 13, 16, 19, ...

   c) 5, 7, 9, 11, 13, ...

   (3 marks)

4 a) Complete the table for $y = 2x - 1$

x	−1	0	2
y			

   (3 marks)

   b) Write down the coordinate pairs for the points. (,   ), (,   ), (,   )

   (3 marks)

   c) On the grid plot the three points.
       Draw and label the line $y = 2x - 1$

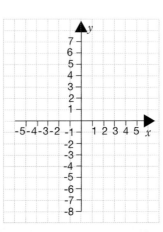

   (2 marks)

d) Explain how you can tell from the graph that the coordinate pair (4, 7) satisfies the rule $y = 2x - 1$

(1 mark)

e) Will (–3, –8) lie on the line? Explain your answer.

(1 mark)

5 Six equations of straight line graphs are written on cards:

| $y = 2x - 3$ | $y = x + 2$ | $y = 3 - 2x$ | $y = 2x + 5$ | $y = 8 + 7x$ | $y = 5 - 4x$ |

If each graph was drawn:

a) Which would have the steepest slope?

b) Which would have a negative slope?

c) Which would cut the y-axis at (0, 3)?

d) Which two would be parallel?

(4 marks)

6 Match these graphs to the statements below:

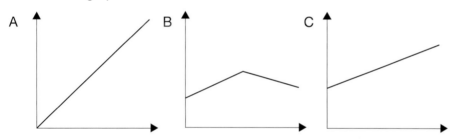

a) The price of petrol started to rise gradually, then fell steadily. ....

b) A mobile phone company charges a standard fee plus a certain amount per call. ....

c) Conversion between kilometres and miles. ....

(3 marks)

(Total 35 marks)

All angles

You want to design a new wallpaper for your room and would like it to have different shapes. You experiment with <u>triangles</u> and <u>quadrilaterals</u>.

1   There are 6 different types of triangles:

<u>scalene</u> – 3 different sides and 3 different angles

<u>equilateral</u> – 3 equal sides and 3 equal angles

<u>isosceles</u> – 2 equal sides and 2 equal angles

<u>right angled</u> – includes 1 right angle

<u>acute-angled</u> – 3 acute angles

<u>obtuse-angled</u> – includes 1 obtuse angle

2   A general quadrilateral is a 4-sided shape with 4 sides and angles.

There are six different types of quadrilateral:

<u>square</u> – 4 equal sides and 4 angles (right angles of 90°)

<u>rectangle</u> – 2 pairs of equal, parallel sides and 4 right angles

<u>parallelogram</u> – 2 pairs of equal, parallel sides and opposite angles equal

<u>rhombus</u> – 4 equal sides, 2 pairs parallel sides and opposite angles equal

<u>trapezium</u> – 1 pair of parallel sides

<u>kite</u> – 2 pairs of adjacent sides equal and 1 pair of opposite angles equal

Fill the gaps

1 These diagrams have pairs of parallel lines crossing each other. One angle in each drawing is given to you. You will find the other marked angles in this key. Write each angle in the correct place and cross it off on the key.

a) 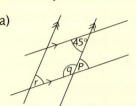 b) 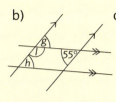 c)

45°	55°	55°	115°	45°
125°	65°	115°	135°	

• TOP TIPS •

1 When you measure angles with a protractor, make sure one arm of the angle is lined up with the 0°–180° base line and that the cross at the centre of this line is on the vertex of the angle.

2 Parallel lines never meet. They stay the same distance apart at all times.

2 Each of these triangles has an extended side, forming an exterior angle. One angle in each triangle, plus the exterior angle, is given to you. You will find the other marked angles in this key. Write each angle in the correct place and cross it off on the key.

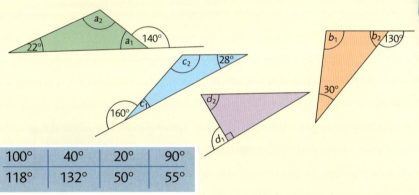

100°	40°	20°	90°
118°	132°	50°	55°

a) The exterior angle is the .... of the 2 opposite interior angles.

b) The exterior angle and adjacent interior angle add up to ....

KEY FACTS

⬆ **There are four main types of angle:**
 (i) <u>acute</u> – between 0° and 90°
 (ii) <u>right angle</u> – 90°
 (iii) <u>obtuse</u> – between 90° and 180°
 (iv) <u>reflex</u> – between 180° and 360°

➡ Angles adding up to 90° are called <u>complementary</u>. Angles adding up to 180° are called <u>supplementary</u>.

⬆ When two lines cross, the <u>opposite</u> angles are equal. The sum of angles at a point is 360°.
➡ When a transversal cuts parallel lines:
 (i) <u>alternate</u> angles (a) are equal
 (ii) <u>corresponding</u> angles (c) are equal
 (iii) <u>interior</u> angles (i) are supplementary

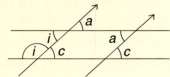

Where did the birdie go?

A bird is nesting on a tall tree. A dog sees the bird and starts barking.

The bird is frightened and flies on a <u>bearing</u> of 050° to the church tower in the next village, which is 24 km away. The church clock strikes 3 o'clock and the bird flies away on a bearing of 160° to a roof 20 km away. Use a scale drawing to find the journey distance and bearing for the bird's return to its nest.

To find the journey distance:

1 Mark a point (nest) with a vertical line for North. Use your protractor to measure 50° in a clockwise direction from the North line.

2 Draw a faint line at an angle 50° clockwise from the North line.

3 Choose a convenient scale, say 1 cm representing 4 km, and measure 6 cm (24 ÷ 4) along your line. At this point (tower), draw another vertical North line.

4 Now measure 160° in a clockwise direction from North.

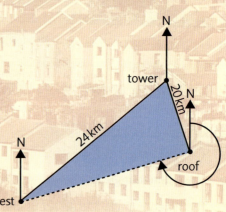

5 Draw a faint line at an angle 160° clockwise from the North line.

6 Mark a point (roof) 5 cm (20 ÷ 4) along your line.

7 Join the roof point to the nest point.

8 Measure this line (6.5 cm) and multiply by 4(6.5 × 4) giving an actual distance of 26 km.

To measure the bearing:

1 Draw another vertical North line at the roof point.

2 Measure the angle between this and the line joining the roof point to the nest point. This is 83°.

3 Subtract this from 360°, giving 277°, which is the bearing for the bird's return journey.

Compass puzzles

This is a picture of a magnetic compass with North marked.

1 Learn the positions of the main compass points.

2 Remember to give each bearing as a three-digit number, e.g. 025°, 167°, 226°.

1 Mark the other three main compass points (S, E, W) on the diagram. Now mark the intermediate points (NE, SE, SW, NW).

2 Fill in the smaller angles on the compass between the following compass points.

   a) N and E

   b) N and W

   c) N and S

   d) E and W

   e) N and SE

   f) S and NE

   g) SE and NW

   h) S and SW

3 Make a scale drawing to illustrate the journey of a ship sailing 25 km from port A on a bearing of 085° and then 30 km due East to port B. If it sails directly back to A, how far is the return journey and on what bearing must it sail?

KEY FACTS

⬆ It is helpful to draw a rough sketch before you do the scale drawing.

➡ Choose a convenient scale and remember to change your scaled lengths back to actual distances.

⬇ Always measure bearings in a clockwise direction from a vertical North line.

⬆ If the angle is reflex and therefore too large for your protractor, measure the other angle and subtract it from 360°.

BEN

Follow that path

A dog is tied, by its lead, to a ring that can slide up and down a vertical pole fixed in the middle of the garden.

1 **Draw the path traced by the dog if the lead is stretched taut.** What shape is the path? A path that follows a specific rule is called a <u>locus</u> (plural: loci).

The dog moves at a given distance (the length of his lead) from a fixed point (the vertical pole). This describes a <u>circle</u> with the pole as centre and <u>radius</u> equal to the length of the lead.

2 One day the pole is turned through a right angle so that it is horizontal. There is a block at both ends so that the ring cannot come off the pole.

3 **Draw the new path traced by the dog if the lead is stretched taut.**

The dog moves at a given distance (the length of its lead) from two fixed points (the ends of the horizontal pole). It also walks in a straight line, either side of the pole and parallel to it.

4 One corner of the garden has two hedges that include an angle of 80°. Now the dog walks in a straight line from the corner, so that it is <u>equidistant</u> from the two hedges.

Draw the path traced by the dog.

5 The dog moves so that it is the same distance from each hedge.

What relation does this path have with the angle between the hedges?

The locus of the path the dog takes is the line <u>bisecting</u> the angle between the hedges.

6 There are two apple trees in the garden. They are 4 metres apart. The dog walks in a straight line, so that it is equidistant from the two trees.

Draw the path traced by the dog.

7 The dog moves so that it is the same distance from each tree.

When the dog is level with the trees, what distance is it from each of them?

The locus of the dog's path is a <u>perpendicular</u> line bisecting the line joining the two trees. This is known as a perpendicular bisector.

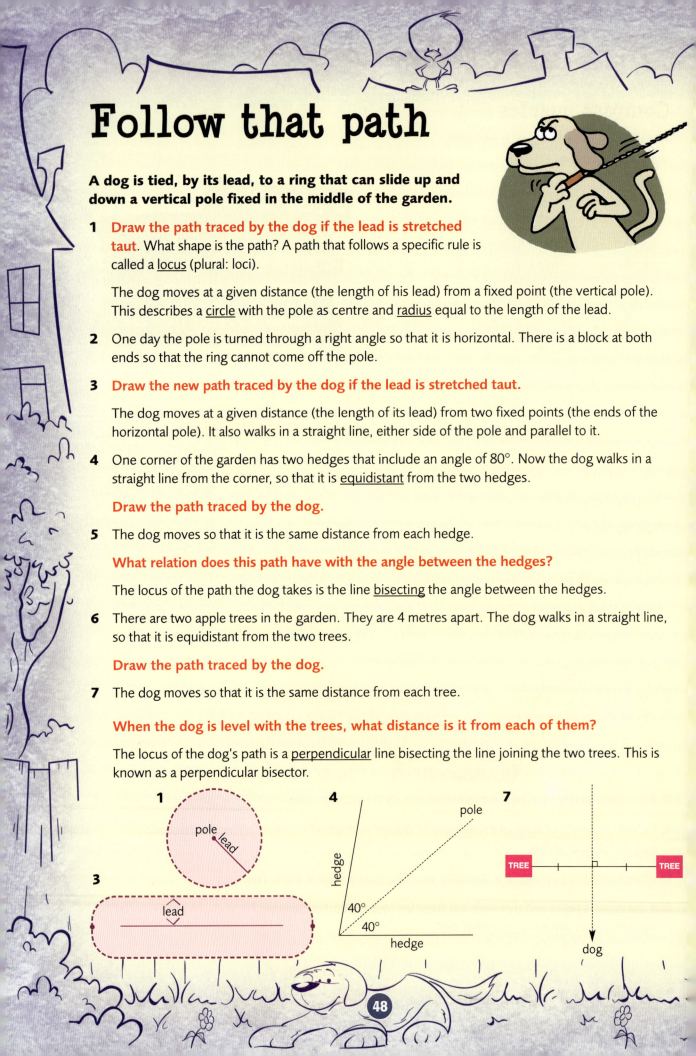

Construction problems

1 This is a plan of a living room. New power points (P) are placed either side of the sofa, for lamps, and in the corner, for a lamp and the television. The lamps give out light over a distance of 1 metre.

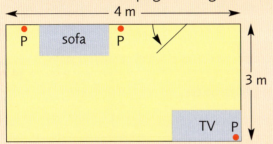

a) Copy the plan and draw the locus of light from each power point.
b) Draw the locus of possible positions for a lamp equidistant from the two sofa lamps.
c) Suggest a position for a further power point in the room.

2 A dog walks at a constant distance of 1.5 metres from a wall. Draw the locus of its path.

3 Construct the locus of the end of a windscreen wiper, length 72 cm.

4 A flowerbed is in the shape of an isosceles triangle with base 2.4 metres. The angle opposite the base is 40°. A gardener is going to plant bulbs in lines equidistant from each pair of sides.

a) Construct the locus of each line of bulbs. Use B to mark the point where they intersect.
b) Measure the distance of B from each vertex.

• TOP TIPS •

1 You will need a sharp pencil, ruler, protractor and a pair of compasses to construct and measure loci.

2 Imagine you are walking along the path described. It will help you draw a locus.

3 Remember to write down the scale you are using when constructing a locus or diagram.

KEY FACTS

⬆ There are 4 main types of loci. A path may be a combination of two or more of these.

(i) The locus of a point moving at a fixed distance (radius) from a fixed point (centre) is a circle.

(ii) The locus of a point moving at a constant distance d from a straight line XY is a pair of lines, either side of and parallel to XY and each at a distance d from it.

(iii) The locus of a point moving so that it is equidistant from two fixed points, X and Y, is the perpendicular bisector of XY.

(iv) The locus of a point moving equidistant from two lines is the bisector of the angle between the lines.

Test your knowledge 6

1   Find the values of x in the diagrams below.

a) 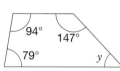   b)   c) 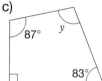   d)

(4 marks)

2   Find the value of angle y in each of the diagrams below.

a) 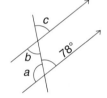   b) 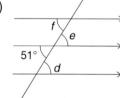   c)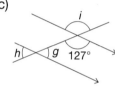

(3 marks)

3   Find the size of the marked angles.

a)   b)   c)

(9 marks)

4   Find the size of the angles marked with the letters.

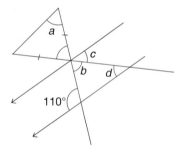

(4 marks)

5   A ship leaves port A and sails on a bearing of 050° for 80 km to port B. It leaves port B and sails on a bearing of 130° for 60 km to port C.

a)   Draw an accurate scale drawing of the journey, using a scale of 1 cm = 10 km.

(2 marks)

b)   Measure the direct distance of port A from port C .... km.

(1 mark)

c)   Measure the bearing of port C from port A ....

(1 mark)

6

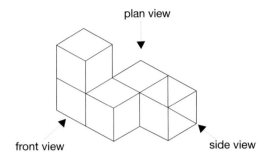

plan view

front view   side view

For the above 3D shape, draw the views from the top, front and side.

plan view   front elevation   side elevation

(3 marks)

7 A beacon transmits radio waves a distance of 4 km. Using a scale of 1 cm = 1 km, draw accurately the locus of the radio waves from the beacon.

• Beacon

(2 marks)

(Total 29 marks)

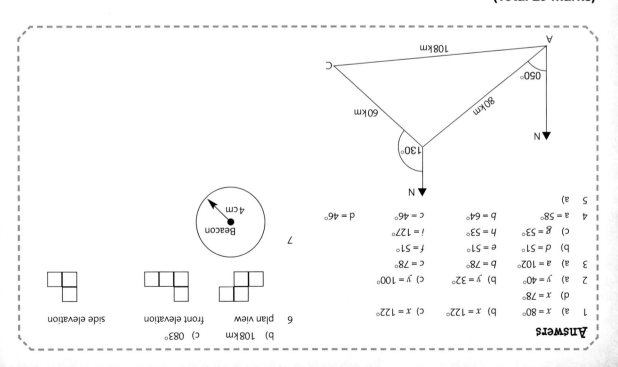

What a transformation!

A gardener wants to design some flowerbeds. He draws axes on squared paper and draws a flowerbed in the first quadrant.

He then transforms it by:

a reflection in the *x*-axis

b rotation through 180° in a clockwise direction about the origin

c translation by a vector ($\frac{-4}{2}$)

d enlargement with centre (0, 2) and scale factor 2

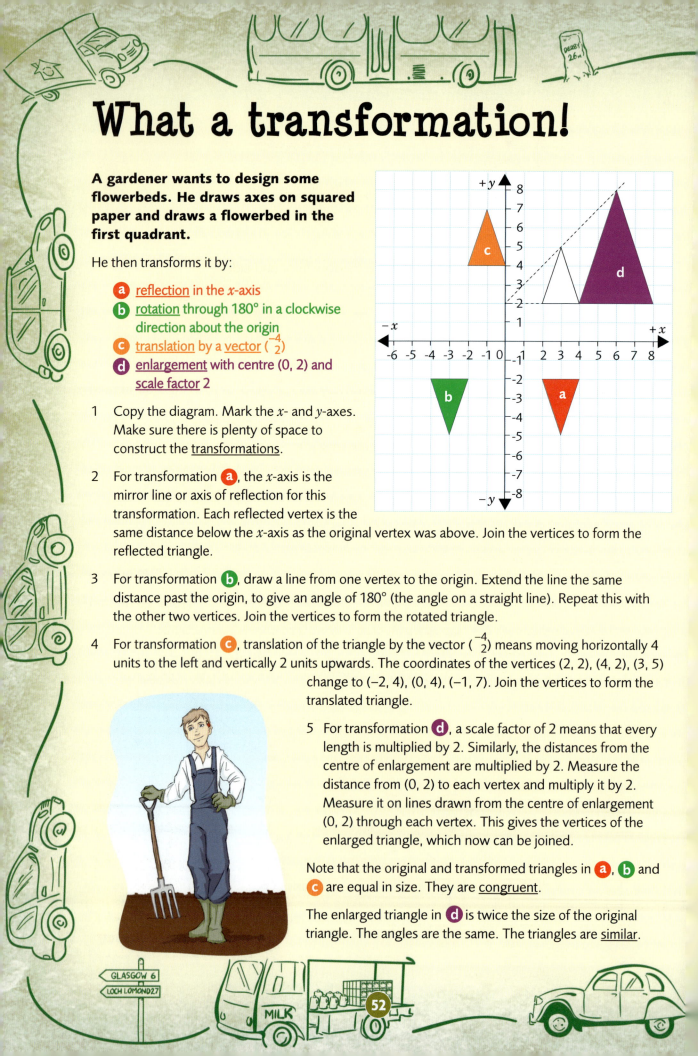

1   Copy the diagram. Mark the *x*- and *y*-axes. Make sure there is plenty of space to construct the transformations.

2   For transformation **a**, the *x*-axis is the mirror line or axis of reflection for this transformation. Each reflected vertex is the same distance below the *x*-axis as the original vertex was above. Join the vertices to form the reflected triangle.

3   For transformation **b**, draw a line from one vertex to the origin. Extend the line the same distance past the origin, to give an angle of 180° (the angle on a straight line). Repeat this with the other two vertices. Join the vertices to form the rotated triangle.

4   For transformation **c**, translation of the triangle by the vector ($\frac{-4}{2}$) means moving horizontally 4 units to the left and vertically 2 units upwards. The coordinates of the vertices (2, 2), (4, 2), (3, 5) change to (−2, 4), (0, 4), (−1, 7). Join the vertices to form the translated triangle.

5   For transformation **d**, a scale factor of 2 means that every length is multiplied by 2. Similarly, the distances from the centre of enlargement are multiplied by 2. Measure the distance from (0, 2) to each vertex and multiply it by 2. Measure it on lines drawn from the centre of enlargement (0, 2) through each vertex. This gives the vertices of the enlarged triangle, which now can be joined.

Note that the original and transformed triangles in **a**, **b** and **c** are equal in size. They are congruent.

The enlarged triangle in **d** is twice the size of the original triangle. The angles are the same. The triangles are similar.

GLASGOW 6

LOCH LOMOND 27

MILK

Transformation puzzles

1 Suppose you want to design wallpaper for your room. You start with squared paper.

   a) You draw a parallelogram with its diagonals. You rotate the shape about the point where the diagonals intersect. What order of rotation symmetry does it have?

   b) You draw a rhombus and translate it by vector $\binom{3}{-2}$.

   c) You draw a square and enlarge it by scale factor 3.

   Draw these transformations.

2 A girl writes her name, Isabella, in capital letters. She reflects them in a mirror placed on a horizontal line.

   ISABELLA

   ....

   a) Copy this and reflect the letters in the line.

   b) Which letters do not change?

   c) Repeat this with your name.

KEY FACTS

⬆ An object has symmetry if it can be folded along a line to give two equal parts fitting exactly over one another.

➡ Reflection of an object in a line or axis of symmetry produces an equal reversed image as in a mirror. The object and image are congruent.

⬇ A shape has rotation symmetry if there are several positions a shape can take, when rotated, and it still looks the same. The number of positions is the order of rotation symmetry. The object and image are congruent.

⬆ Translation moves a shape to another position. A vector is used to describe the distances moved. The object and image are congruent.

⬅ Enlargement makes a shape larger by a given scale factor multiplying each length. If the scale factor is less than 1, the image will be smaller than the object. The object and image are similar.

• TOP TIPS •

1 Give the line of symmetry for reflection.

2 Give direction, angle and centre for rotation.

3 Give the vector for translation.

4 Give the scale factor and centre for enlargement.

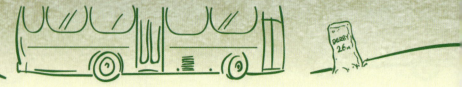

How far to go?

Suppose you live in Cambridge and you have friends in Edinburgh, Leeds, Newcastle, Portsmouth and London. One summer holiday, you decide to visit them all. Before deciding how to travel, you draw up a table of distances between the cities. The distances are measured in miles.

Cambridge					
326	Edinburgh				
144	190	Leeds			
232	104	96	Newcastle		
132	448	245	360	Portsmouth	
58	373	196	278	74	London

What is the distance between these cities in kilometres?

- **Cambridge to London**
  To use the table to find distances in miles, follow row and column until they meet. The Cambridge column meets the London row at 58 miles. As 5 miles equals approximately 8 kilometres, divide 58 by 5 and then multiply by 8 to convert it to kilometres. $(58 \div 5) \times 8 = 92.8\,km$

- **Edinburgh to Portsmouth**
  The Edinburgh column meets the Portsmouth row at 448 miles. $(448 \div 5) \times 8 = 716.8\,km$

- **London to Leeds**
  The London row meets the Leeds column at 196 miles. $(196 \div 5) \times 8 = 313.6\,km$

- **London to Newcastle**
  The London row meets the Newcastle column at 278 miles. $(278 \div 5) \times 8 = 444.8\,km$

You decide to travel from Edinburgh to Portsmouth, via Leeds and London. What is the total distance of your journey?

Your journey is Edinburgh to Leeds, Leeds to London and then London to Portsmouth. Add these distances in miles, then convert to kilometres.

$$190 + 196 + 74 = 460 \text{ miles} \rightarrow (460 \div 5) \times 8 = 736\,km$$

If a litre of petrol costs 81.5p and your car uses 1 litre of petrol for every 14km it travels, how much petrol would be used on the journey from Edinburgh to Portsmouth, via Leeds and London?

The car uses 1 litre of petrol for every 14km it travels. Divide 736 by 14. Then multiply the answer by the cost of a litre of petrol.

$$(736 \div 14) \times 81.5p = (736 \div 14) \times £0.815 = £42.84571429$$

As cost in £ must always have 2 decimal places, the cost of petrol for the journey is £42.85.

Finding the measure

1 Fill in these areas in the given units.

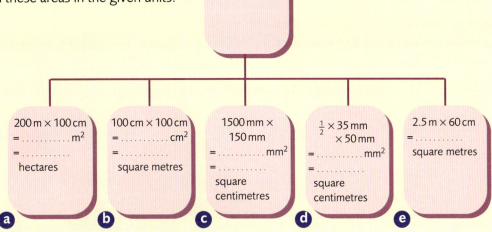

Changing units

a
200 m × 100 cm
= .... m²
= ....
hectares

b
100 cm × 100 cm
= .... cm²
= ....
square metres

c
1500 mm × 150 mm
= .... mm²
= ....
square centimetres

d
$\frac{1}{2}$ × 35 mm × 50 mm
= .... mm²
= ....
square centimetres

e
2.5 m × 60 cm
= ....
square metres

2 This is a recipe for ginger cake in <u>imperial</u> units.

1 lb self-raising flour	$\frac{1}{2}$ lb sugar
1 lb golden syrup	$\frac{1}{2}$ pt milk
4 tsp ginger	2 eggs
2 tsp cinnamon	1 tsp bicarbonate of soda
$\frac{1}{2}$ lb margarine	

Rewrite the recipe, converting quantities to metric units where appropriate.

3 A girl's watch is digital, so it is based on the 24-hour clock. The kitchen clock is in 12-hour clock time.

Complete this table, converting the times from one clock to the other.

	kitchen clock	girl's watch
a)	10.15am	
b)		0015
c)	6.35pm	
d)		2020

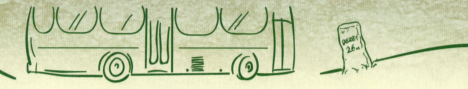

Cartons, containers & crates

Imagine that you're having a party and want to buy some cartons of fruit juice. Cartons of orange juice measure 14.5 cm by 7 cm by 4 cm. There are 20 cartons in each container.

a How much orange juice is in each carton?

The <u>capacity</u> of a carton is found by calculating its <u>volume</u>. To calculate a volume, multiply height by width by depth.

$$14.5 \times 7 \times 4 = 406 \, cm^3$$

b What are the dimensions of the container?

Twenty cartons can be fitted in a container by having two rows of five in each layer and two layers.

∴ Dimensions are 35 cm by 29 cm by 8 cm.

c What is the volume of the container?

The volume of a container is found by multiplying height by width by depth.

$$35 \times 29 \times 8 = 8120 \, cm^3$$

d What area of card is used for each container?

The area of card needed for a container is its <u>surface area</u>. The container is a cuboid. To find the surface area of a cuboid, calculate the area of each face (side) and add them. There are three pairs of equal faces.

Surface area of container $= 2[(35 \times 29) + (29 \times 8) + (8 \times 35)] = 2[1015 + 232 + 280]$

$$= 2 \times 1527 = 3054 \, cm^2$$

e There are three containers in each crate.

(i) What are the dimensions of the crate?

Three containers can be fitted into a crate by placing three in a pile.

∴ Dimensions are 35 cm by 29 cm by 24 cm.

(ii) What is the volume of the crate?

The volume of a crate is found by multiplying height by width by depth.

$$35 \times 29 \times 24 = 24360 \, cm^3$$

Container puzzles

There are different sizes of cartons of cereal on the kitchen shelf.

a) Flakies cereal, which comes in two different sizes of carton measuring:

 • 24 cm by 17.4 cm by 5 cm costing £1.34

 • 25.8 cm by 19 cm by 6 cm costing £1.96

b) A variety pack of eight small cartons, each measuring 103 mm by 70 mm by 37 mm costing £2.99.

1 Write the capacity and surface area on each carton.

2 The capacity of the whole variety pack is .... cm^3.

3 A whole variety pack needs .... cm^2 of cardboard.

4 The Flakies carton measuring .... is better value.

5 .... is most expensive for each cm^2.

Test your knowledge 7

1 On the grid opposite:

    a) Reflect triangle A in the x-axis. Call the new shape B.

    b) Translate triangle A 5 squares to the left and 2 squares upwards. Call the new shape C.

    c) Rotate triangle A 180° about the origin. Call the new shape D.

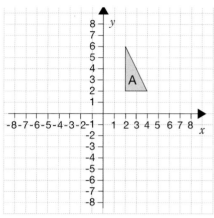

(6 marks)

2 On the grid opposite, enlarge shape N with a scale factor of 2, centre of enlargement at (0, 0).

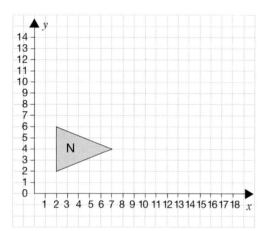

(2 marks)

3 Change the following measurements.

    a) 400 mm to m   b) 1265 g to kg

    c) 5020 kg to tonnes   d) 2.72 l to cl

(4 marks)

4 A petrol tank holds 4050 cl of petrol.

    a) How many litres does the tank hold?

    b) What is the volume of the tank in cm^3?

(2 marks)

5 A book measures 28 cm by 15 cm. Find the appropriate dimensions of this book in inches.

(2 marks)

6 Calculate the area of these shapes.

a)

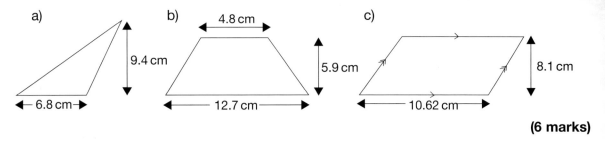

9.4 cm

6.8 cm

b)

4.8 cm

5.9 cm

12.7 cm

c)

8.1 cm

10.62 cm

(6 marks)

7 The area of this triangle is 12 cm^2. The base is 4.2 cm. What is the height of this triangle? (Give your answer to 2 decimal places.)

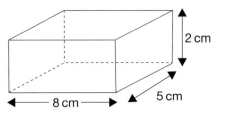

Area = 12 cm^2

4.2 cm

(2 marks)

8 For the cuboid opposite, calculate

a) the volume

b) the total surface area

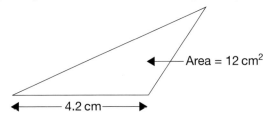

2 cm

8 cm

5 cm

(4 marks)

(Total 28 marks)

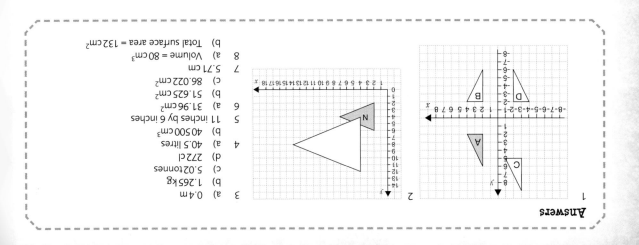

Turn the tables

Imagine that you would like to know the average number of tracks on a CD and the average length of a track.

You could work out the information in three ways.

(i) You could look at a selection of your CDs, checking the number of tracks and the length of each one. This would be a <u>sample</u>. You would need to record this in a <u>data</u> collection sheet, so that you could analyse it later. This is an example of a <u>primary source</u> of data.

CD	Number of tracks	Length of track

(ii) You could look at all your CDs, checking the number of tracks and the length of each one. You could use a <u>tally</u> chart to record your findings, making sure that you calculated the frequencies in a separate column. This is also an example of a primary source of data.

(iii) You could use the Internet, catalogues of CDs, or contact recording companies to find the information you need. You could again use tallying to record your findings, calculating frequencies in a separate column. This is called a <u>frequency</u> table. As you would not have found this data yourself, it is known as a <u>secondary source</u> of data.

Number of tracks	Tally	Frequency

or

Length of track	Tally	Frequency

You could combine in a <u>two-way table</u> with columns for the track lengths (to nearest 30 seconds), and rows for the number of tracks.

No. of tracks	2 minutes	2.5 minutes	3 minutes	3.5 minutes	4 minutes	4.5 minutes	5 minutes +
≤15							
16–19							
20–24							
≥25							

What's the data?

The local travel agent wants to find out where people like to stay when they go on holiday. He surveys three groups: 18–25 year-olds, families and 55+. The following data collection sheets show the results of his surveys.

(key: C/C = camping/caravan; SC = self-catering; B&B = bed & breakfast; H = hotel)

a) 18–25

SC	C/C	SC	B&B	C/C	B&B	C/C	SC	SC	SC
C/C	B&B	C/C	B&B	C/C	SC	SC	C/C	H	SC
C/C	C/C	B&B	C/C	SC	SC	C/C	SC	SC	H
B&B	C/C	C/C	B&B	C/C	C/C	SC	SC	SC	C/C
B&B	SC	H	B&B	B&B	C/C	C/C	SC	SC	C/C

b) families

SC	C/C	SC	B&B	C/C	H	C/C	SC	SC	SC
C/C	B&B	C/C	SC	SC	SC	SC	C/C	H	SC
C/C	C/C	B&B	C/C	SC	SC	C/C	SC	SC	H
H	C/C	C/C	B&B	C/C	C/C	SC	SC	SC	C/C
B&B	SC	H	B&B	B&B	C/C	C/C	SC	SC	C/C

c) 55+

B&B	C/C	SC	B&B	C/C	B&B	H	SC	B&B	B&B
C/C	B&B	C/C	B&B	H	SC	SC	H	H	H
C/C	C/C	B&B	H	H	SC	H	B&B	SC	H
B&B	H	H	B&B	C/C	H	SC	SC	B&B	H
B&B	H	H	B&B	B&B	H	C/C	SC	SC	B&B

1   Complete the tallying and frequency for each survey in this table.

18–25 holiday	tally	freq.	family holiday	tally	freq.	55+ holiday	tally	freq.
C/C			C/C			C/C		
SC			SC			SC		
B&B			B&B			B&B		
H			H			H		

2   18–25 sample size = ... families sample size = ...
55+ sample size =............... .

3   This data is a .... source.

4   The travel agent could obtain the other type of data using ....,
.... and ....

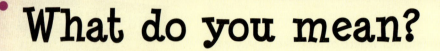

What do you mean?

Imagine each person in your science class has planted a sunflower seed to see whose plant grows to be the tallest. After some time, you measure and record the various heights of the 30 sunflowers.

135 cm	128 cm	118 cm	117 cm	145 cm	132 cm
112 cm	134 cm	130 cm	116 cm	124 cm	141 cm
129 cm	133 cm	107 cm	127 cm	125 cm	108 cm
136 cm	127 cm	109 cm	110 cm	125 cm	133 cm
138 cm	120 cm	140 cm	122 cm	139 cm	127 cm

- These measurements can be organised into a stem-and-leaf diagram.

  A stem-and-leaf diagram is used for displaying data. The 'tens' digits form the stem and the 'units' digits form the leaves.

10	7	8	9							
11	0	2	6	7	8					
12	0	2	4	5	5	7	7	7	8	9
13	0	2	3	3	4	5	6	8	9	
14	0	1	5							

- You can calculate (i) the mean height, (ii) the median height, (iii) the modal height, (iv) the range of heights as follows:

  (i) Find the mean by adding all items of data and dividing by the number of items. The mean height is 126.23 cm (3787 ÷ 30).

  (ii) Before finding the median, arrange the data in ascending order of size. This is already done in the stem-and-leaf diagram. If the number of items is odd, the median is the middle item, but in this case there are 30 items, which is an even number. The middle item lies between the 15th and 16th items. They are both 127 cm, so this is the median. If they were different, the median would be the mean of the two values.

  (iii) The mode is the most frequently occuring item. From the stem-and-leaf diagram, you can see that this is 127 cm, so this is the modal height.

  (iv) The range is found by subtracting the smallest quantity from the largest quantity. The range of heights is 38 cm (145 cm – 107 cm).

- Which is the most appropriate average to use?

  The median and mode are the same (127 cm). The mean is less than a centimetre below them. The most appropriate average is the mode as it is the easiest to measure.

Data puzzles

1 You have an appointment in town T. You have to be there by 1430. You need to travel by train from the local station S, via station V, to T. This timetable shows the trains you could use.

Depart S	08 47	09 47	10 47	11 47	12 47
Arrive V	09 32	10 30	11 32	12 30	13 35
Arrive T	10 12	11 07	12 12	13 10	14 15
Journey time					

   a) Fill in the journey times on the timetable. Tick the correct range:

   5 minutes   8 minutes   10 minutes

   b) mean journey time = ... hour .... minutes
   median journey time = ... hour .... minutes

   c) Tick the more reliable average.   mean ☐   median ☐

   d) You should use the .... train, because of ....

2 A boy in your class brings nuts in his packed lunch every day. This table shows how many he eats in a particular week at home and school.

Day	Sun	Mon	Tues	Wed	Thurs	Fri	Sat
Number of biscuits	6	5	6	8	3	5	6

   a) The mean number of nuts he eats each day is ....

   b) mode = ... median = ... range = ...

3 The English test marks for a Year 8 class are shown in this table.

53	52	87	70	75	80	45	43	93	55	51	22
35	45	63	65	83	79	42	68	50	78	67	90
44	38	50	58	39	60	60	39	80	18	45	30
64	29	80	18	72	36	55	37	43	49	40	60
65	37	43	59	29	41	75	72	70	35	29	60

   a) Organise the marks into a stem-and-leaf diagram.

   b) mean = ... median = ... modal mark = ...

   c) .... is the most appropriate average to use
   because ....

• TOP TIPS •

When you are finding the median, remember to arrange data in ascending order before picking out the middle value.

KEY FACTS

⬆ **There are three averages:**

(i) **mean** – to find this, add items of data and divide by the number of items.

(ii) **median** – this is the middle value when an odd number of data items is arranged in ascending order; and the mean of the two middle values when an even number of data items is arranged in ascending order.

(iii) **mode** – this is the most frequent item of data.

➡ **The range of values is the difference between the largest and smallest items of data.**

Is there a dog in that window?

Imagine that your local vet has done a survey of the pet-owning households in the area. This table shows the results.

Pet	Bird	Cat	Dog	Fish	Gerbil	Rabbit	Pony
Frequency	2	8	7	15	5	3	5

You can illustrate this data by drawing:

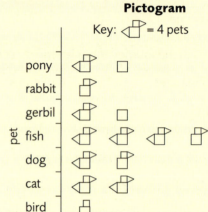

Pictogram

- a <u>pictogram</u>
  A pictogram uses small pictures or symbols to represent a number of items. A key must be given to explain how many items the symbol represents. Choose something simple.

- a <u>bar chart</u>
  A bar chart uses horizontal or vertical bars or columns of equal width to represent data. Frequency is given by length or height of bars.

- a <u>pie chart</u>
  A pie chart represents data in a circle divided into sections. The size of each section is given by the angle at the centre. This is calculated by dividing 360° by the total frequency. This gives the angle for a single item. In this case, $\frac{360°}{45} = 8°$. Multiply each frequency by this angle.

Pet	Bird	Cat	Dog	Fish	Gerbil	Rabbit	Pony
Frequency	2	8	7	15	5	3	5
Pie chart angle	2 × 8° =16°	8 × 8° = 64°	7 × 8° = 56°	15 × 8° = 120°	5 × 8° = 40°	3 × 8° = 24°	5 × 8° = 40°

The total of the angles should be 360°.

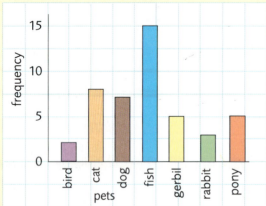

Bar chart

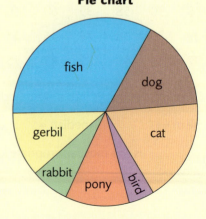

Pie chart

Making the charts

Esther comes home from school with her test results in Maths, English, French and Science. Her marks are in the first column in this table. She is part of a sample of six pupils from her school year.

subject	Esther	pupil A	pupil B	pupil C	pupil D	pupil E
English	50	56	75	60	48	55
French	45	46	60	60	50	35
Maths	45	72	65	30	33	52
Science	40	65	60	35	25	45

a) Draw a <u>compound bar chart</u> comparing the English and French marks.

b) Comment on the relationship between the English and French marks.

c) Draw a pie chart to illustrate Esther's marks. What do you notice about her marks in these four subjects?

d) Draw a pictogram to illustrate the sample Science marks.

KEY FACTS

⬆ **A pictogram uses small pictures or symbols (which are described in a key) to represent a number of items.**

➡ **A bar chart uses horizontal or vertical bars or columns of equal width to represent data. Frequency is given by length or height of bars.**

⬇ **A compound bar chart illustrates two or more sets of data using different colour bars on the same axes.**

⬆ **A pie chart represents data in a circle. It is divided into slices. The size of each slice is calculated by dividing 360° by the total frequency to give the angle for a single item. Each frequency is multiplied by this angle.**

• TOP TIPS •

1 Choose a simple picture or symbol for your pictogram.

2 It is usual to leave gaps between bars in a bar chart. You can just use vertical or horizontal lines.

3 Remember to check that the angles in a pie chart add up to 360°.

Test your knowledge 8

1   This table shows the hair colour of the boys and girls in Ahmed's class.

	Girls	Boys
Black	3	4
Blonde	6	3
Red	1	0
Brown	6	9

    a)   How many brown-haired boys were in Ahmed's class?   **(1 mark)**

    b)   How many girls were in the class?   **(1 mark)**

    c)   How many blonde-haired pupils were in the class?   **(1 mark)**

2   The data shows the scores out of 10 for some students in a spelling test.

$$7, 4, 7, 2, 9, 7, 7, 5, 5, 2$$

Calculate

    a)   The mean score.   **(2 marks)**

    b)   The median score.   **(1 mark)**

    c)   The range.   **(1 mark)**

    d)   The mode.   **(1 mark)**

3   The table shows the number of goals scored by a football team.

Number of goals	0	1	2	3	4	5
Frequency	12	14	6	4	7	1

Use a calculator to work out the mean number of goals.

    (2 marks)

4   Find the median, range and mode from this stem-and-leaf diagram:

Marks out of 50 in a test

```
0 | 8                        stem = tens
1 | 1  4  7  9               leaf = units
2 | 2  2  7  7  7  9
3 | 1  1  5  6
4 | 6  6  8
5 | 0
```

    (3 marks)

5 The table shows the time in minutes that shoppers had to wait at the supermarket checkout.

On the grid below draw a frequency diagram for this table.

Time (*t*) in minutes	frequency
$0 \leqslant t < 2$	4
$2 \leqslant t < 4$	6
$4 \leqslant t \leqslant 6$	7
$6 \leqslant t < 8$	2
$8 \leqslant t < 10$	1

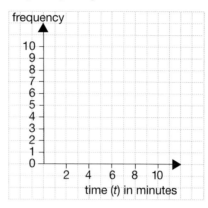

(2 marks)

6 The table shows the colour of some cars in a car park.

Colour	Silver	Blue	Red	Black
Frequency	6	4	10	4

Draw a pie chart of this information in the circle below:

(4 marks)

(Total 19 marks)

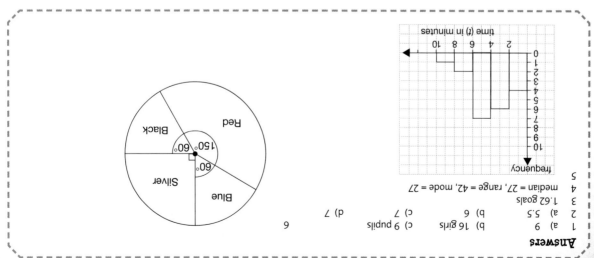
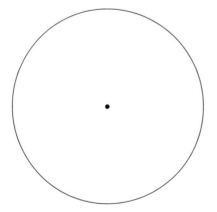

The cost of age

Tom's parents are car dealers. They have kept an account of the value of their cars as they get older. They have drawn a <u>scatter graph</u> to illustrate this data. A scatter graph is used to compare two variables, plotting one set of data against another. If there is a relationship between them it is called <u>correlation</u>.

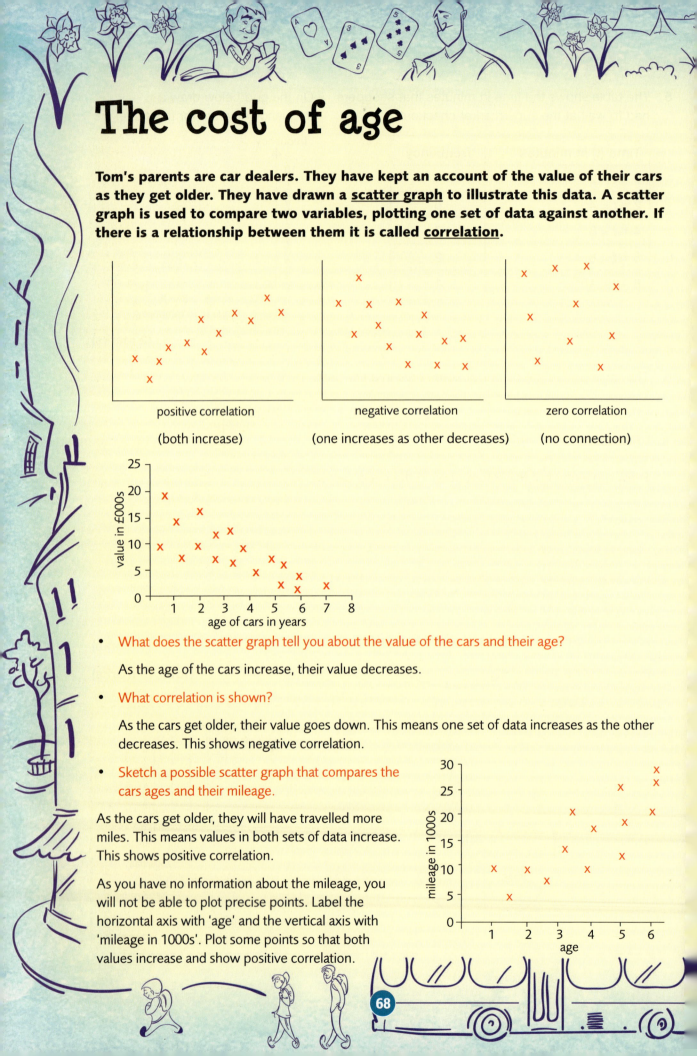

positive correlation

(both increase)

negative correlation

(one increases as other decreases)

zero correlation

(no connection)

- What does the scatter graph tell you about the value of the cars and their age?

As the age of the cars increase, their value decreases.

- What correlation is shown?

As the cars get older, their value goes down. This means one set of data increases as the other decreases. This shows negative correlation.

- Sketch a possible scatter graph that compares the cars ages and their mileage.

As the cars get older, they will have travelled more miles. This means values in both sets of data increase. This shows positive correlation.

As you have no information about the mileage, you will not be able to plot precise points. Label the horizontal axis with 'age' and the vertical axis with 'mileage in 1000s'. Plot some points so that both values increase and show positive correlation.

Conversions

1 You intend to take a touring holiday in a few European countries. They all use the euro (€). You are given a <u>conversion graph</u> to help you convert money into € when you are on holiday.

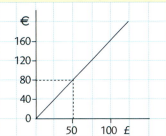

Complete these statements:

a) £50 = ... €   £100 = ... €   £1000 = ... €

b) 50€...... = £......   100€...... = £......   200€...... = £ ......

2 A group of friends are comparing how they spend their weekly allowance. They average out the results and draw a pie chart for the girls and a bar chart for the boys.

boys **girls**

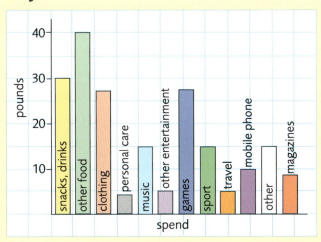

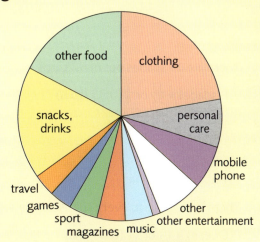

Use the charts to fill in this two-way table.

	Boys	Girls
Weekly allowance		£21
Clothing		
Sports		
Magazines		

KEY FACTS

⬆ Use a scatter graph to compare two sets of data.

➡ The connection or relationship between these sets of data is called correlation; positive if they both increase and negative if one increases while the other decreases.

⬇ If values in both sets of data increase, there is positive correlation.

⬆ If values in one set increase as those in the other decrease, there is negative correlation.

Pick a card

Imagine you shuffle a pack of cards and ask a friend to pick a card at random. You want to know the <u>probability</u> of your friend picking a particular card. The probability of something happening is the chance it may happen. Probability lies between 0 (impossible event) and 1 (certain event). If two events cannot happen at the same time, then the P(event not happening) = 1 – P(event happening).

First you need to know the facts about a pack of cards. There are 52 playing cards in a pack. This is divided into 4 suits of 13 cards each – spades, hearts, diamonds and clubs. Spades and clubs are black cards. Hearts and diamonds are red cards. Each suit has an Ace (1), cards numbered 2 to 10 and three picture cards. These are Jack, Queen and King.

What is the probability of your friend picking a red card?

Half a pack is red, so there are 26 red cards out of 52 cards.

$\therefore$ P(red card) = $\frac{26}{52}$ or $\frac{1}{2}$ (0.5, 50%)

What is the probability of your friend not picking a red card?

P(not picking red card) = 1 – P(red card) = 1 – $\frac{1}{2}$ = $\frac{1}{2}$ (0.5, 50%)

What is the probability of your friend picking a spade?

There are 13 spades out of 52 cards.

$\therefore$ P(spade) = $\frac{13}{52}$ or $\frac{1}{4}$ (0.25, 25%)

What is the probability of your friend not picking a spade?

P(not picking spade) = 1 – P(spade) = 1 – $\frac{1}{4}$ = $\frac{3}{4}$ (0.75, 75%)

What is the probability of your friend picking a Queen?

There is a Queen in every suit, so there 4 Queens out of 52 cards.

P(Queen) = $\frac{4}{52}$ or $\frac{1}{13}$ (0.08, 8%)

What is the probability of your friend not picking a Queen?

P(not picking Queen) = 1 – P(Queen) = 1 – $\frac{1}{13}$ = $\frac{12}{13}$ (0.92, 92%)

What is the probability of your friend picking a black heart?

The heart suit is red, so it is impossible for your friend to pick a black heart.

$\therefore$ P(black heart) = 0

What is the probability of your friend picking either a red card or a black card?

The pack of cards consists of red or black cards, so your friend is certain to pick either red or black cards.

P(either red card or black card) = 1

How likely is it?

1 Write on each card the probability of picking that letter at random and replacing it.

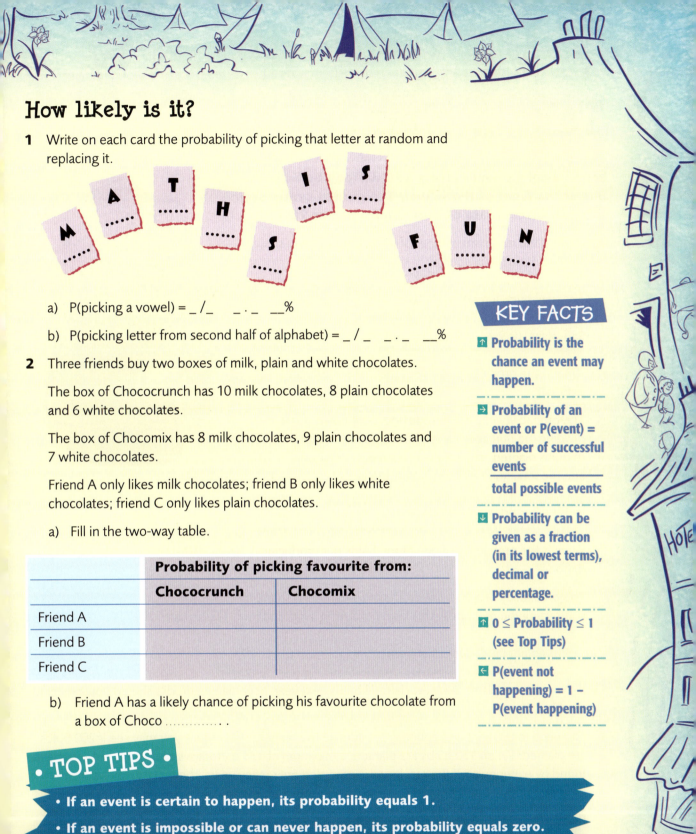

a) P(picking a vowel) = _ /_   _ . _   __%

b) P(picking letter from second half of alphabet) = _ / _   _ . _   __%

2 Three friends buy two boxes of milk, plain and white chocolates.

The box of Chococrunch has 10 milk chocolates, 8 plain chocolates and 6 white chocolates.

The box of Chocomix has 8 milk chocolates, 9 plain chocolates and 7 white chocolates.

Friend A only likes milk chocolates; friend B only likes white chocolates; friend C only likes plain chocolates.

a) Fill in the two-way table.

	Probability of picking favourite from:	
	Chococrunch	Chocomix
Friend A		
Friend B		
Friend C		

b) Friend A has a likely chance of picking his favourite chocolate from a box of Choco ....

• TOP TIPS •

- **If an event is certain to happen, its probability equals 1.**

- **If an event is impossible or can never happen, its probability equals zero.**

- **The probability of all other events lie between 0 and 1 and can be illustrated on a <u>probability scale</u>.**

impossible	equally likely	certain
0	0.5	1

Take a chance

Your school gardener plants 150 daffodil bulbs in a bed at the front of the school. The garden centre says that the success rate of these bulbs is over 90%.

○ What is the minimum number of these daffodils you should expect to see in the spring?

> The minimum number of daffodils you should expect to see in the spring is 90% of 150 bulbs, which equals 135 bulbs. (0.9 x 150 = 135)

○ What is the probability of one of the bulbs producing a daffodil?

The probability of a bulb producing a daffodil is found by dividing the number of successful bulbs by the total number of bulbs planted. The estimated number of daffodils is 135 and the total number of bulbs planted is 150.

> P(bulb producing a daffodil) = $\frac{135}{150}$ = $\frac{9}{10}$ or 0.9 or 90%

○ What is the probability of one of the bulbs not producing a daffodil?

The probability of a bulb not producing a daffodil is found by subtracting the probability of a bulb producing a daffodil from 1 (see pages 70–71).

> P(bulb not producing a daffodil) = $1 - \frac{9}{10} = \frac{1}{10}$ or 0.1 or 10%

○ If the gardener plants 200 new daffodil bulbs next year, how many daffodils should you expect to see from these?

You need to use <u>relative frequency</u> to estimate the number of daffodils you may see if 200 bulbs are planted. When 150 bulbs are planted, a minimum of 135 daffodils is produced. This has been found by experiment. If the results were recorded over many years, the results may be slightly different, but you can compare them with the relative frequency based on the first year's results.

Relative frequency = number of successful bulbs ÷ total number of bulbs planted = $\frac{9}{10}$ or 0.9 or 90% (see above).

> ∴ If 200 bulbs were planted next year, you would expect to see $\frac{9}{10}$ of the 200 bulbs, which is 180 daffodils. [$\frac{9}{10}$ x 200 = 180]

More chances

1 The lottery draw is from numbers 1 to 49.

The following probabilities, of the first ball drawn, are given in a code where digits 0–9 correspond to the last 10 letters of the alphabet, in order.

a) P(even) = SU/UZ = __ /__

b) P(prime) = RV/UZ = __ /__

c) P(factor of 48) = RQ/UZ = __ /__

d) P(multiple of 7) = R/X = __ /__

e) P(number containing a zero) = U/UZ = __ /__

2 Your school canteen has a choice of five lunches.

Burgers	Pasta	Fish and chips	Pizza	Salad
0.22	0.17	0.21	0.27	

These are the predicted theoretical probabilities of pupils choosing burgers, pasta, fish and chips and pizza.

a) Fill in the theoretical probability of choosing salad.

b) Design a questionnaire so that you could find out the actual choices of your school year.

3 There are three ways of finding the probabilities of the outcomes of an event if they are not equally likely.

Calculate theoretical probability	Carry out experiment	Secondary sources of data

Write each of these predictions under the appropriate heading.

a) Your fellow pupils choosing a particular subject for GCSE.
b) Fog on a specific day.
c) A plane being delayed.
d) Hitting the bull's eye on a dartboard.
e) Your dog catching a thrown ball.

Test your knowledge 9

1   The scatter diagram shows the relationship between the number of pairs of gloves sold in a department store and the temperature outside.

The number of pairs of gloves sold is recorded on the same day each week and the temperature that day is noted.

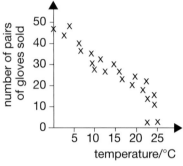

a) What does the scatter diagram show about the relationship between the number of pairs of gloves sold and the temperature outside?   **(1 mark)**

b) Use the scatter diagram to estimate how many pairs of gloves are sold when the temperature is 10 °C.   **(1 mark)**

c) One day the department store sold 24 pairs of gloves. Use the scatter diagram to estimate the temperature.   **(1 mark)**

2   During a survey, pupils in Year 7 and Year 9 were asked to name their favourite subject. The pie charts show the results. There are 160 pupils in Year 7 and 90 pupils in Year 9.

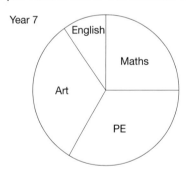

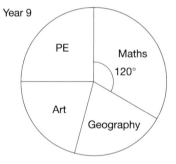

Daisy says 'The charts show that more Year 9 pupils than Year 7 pupils prefer maths as their favourite subject.' Is Daisy correct? Give a reason for your answer.

(2 marks)

3   A bag contains 3 red, 4 blue and 6 green beads.
A bag is drawn out of the bag at random.
What is the probability of choosing:

a) a red bead?   b) a blue bead?   **(2 marks)**

c) a red or green bead?   d) a yellow bead?   **(2 marks)**

4 Archie has an answering machine. If the probability of a caller leaving a message is 0.65, what is the probability that the caller will not leave a message?

(2 marks)

5 The spinner is spun twice. The numbers are added.

a) Complete the sample space diagram.

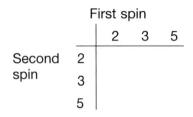

First spin

Second spin	2	3	5
2			
3			
5			

(2 marks)

b) Find the probability that the total will be:

(i) 6 **(1 mark)**

(ii) an even number **(1 mark)**

(iii) a prime number **(1 mark)**

6 205 out of the last 600 cars that passed the school gate were silver. Estimate the probability that the next car to go past will be silver.

(1 mark)

7 The probability of passing a driving test first time is 0.45. On any particular day 200 drivers sit their driving test for the first time. Estimate the number of people who pass their driving test first time on any particular day.

(2 marks)

(Total 19 marks)

Glossary

Algebraic expression A term or group of terms using letters as well as numbers.

Angle The amount of turn, from one direction to another, measured in degrees.

Approximation Nearly correct but not exact.

Area The surface of a shape or object.

Ascending Going up in order from smallest to largest.

Average The amount of flat space occupied by normal or standard amount or value.

Bar chart A chart in which bars of equal width represent statistics.

Bearing Gives the direction of a travelling object. It is measured clockwise, in degrees, from the North line and given as a three-figure angle.

Bias Having a tendency towards some value or away from the normal.

Bisect To bisect is to divide a line, angle or area exactly in half.

BODMAS An acronym that helps you to remember the order of operation. [**B**rackets(**O**rders(powers)(**D**ivision & **M**ultiplication)(**A**ddition & **S**ubtraction)]

Capacity The amount of space in a container or the amount of liquid it will hold.

Circle A shape that has every point on its edge at a fixed distance from its centre.

Common factor Factor that is the same for two or more numbers.

Compass points The four main compass points are the directions North, South, East and West, determined by magnetic north.

Compound bar chart A bar chart used to compare two or more sets of data.

Congruent Congruent shapes can be turned into one another by a rotation, reflection or translation.

Conversion graph A graph used to convert one quantity to another.

Coordinates Pairs of numbers in the form (x, y), giving the position of a point on a graph or grid.

Correlation The connection between two variables, which can be found by drawing a scatter graph.

Data A collection of numbers or information.

Decimal place In a decimal number, the position of a digit after the decimal point.

Decimal point The dot used to separate the whole number from the decimal fraction.

Descending Going down in order from largest to smallest.

Directed number A number with a given sign + or −.

Distance–time graph A graph showing how distance varies with time.

Enlargement A transformation of a figure by a given scale factor.

Equation A mathematical statement showing quantities that are equal.

Equidistant A point the same distance from two or more other points, or lines.

Equivalent fraction One fraction with the same value as another fraction.

Estimation An approximation of the actual value.

Even number A number that, when divided by two, has no remainder.

Experimental probability Probability found by the event being carried out many times.

Factor A whole number that exactly divides another whole number.

Formula An equation used to find quantities when given certain values.

Fraction Part of the whole.

Frequency The number of times that something happens.

Gradient A measure of the slope of a line.

Graph A way of illustrating a relationship between variables.

Highest common factor (HCF) The highest factor common to two or more numbers.

Imperial system Weights and measurements used before the metric system was introduced.

Increase To grow or get bigger. To enlarge or make an addition.

Index The power of a number, indicating the number of times a number is multiplied by itself.

Intercept The point where a line crosses an axis on a graph.

Line of symmetry A line about which a shape is symmetrical.

Locus The path of a point that moves according to a given rule.

Loss How much money is lost by buying something and then selling it at a lower price.

Lowest common denominator Lowest common multiple of all the denominators in a set of fractions.

Lowest common multiple The lowest number that is a multiple of two or more numbers.

Magic square An arrangement of numbers in the form of a square. Each column, row and diagonal has the same sum.

Mean An average value found by dividing the sum of a set of quantities by the number of quantities.

Median The middle item in an ascending or descending sequence of items.

Metric system Based on multiples of 10.

Mode An average value that is the most frequent value.

Multiple If a number divides exactly into another number, the second is a multiple of the first.

Negative number A number less than zero.

Nth term The general term of a number sequence.

Number pattern A pattern followed by a set of numbers.

Odd number A number, that, when divided by 2, gives a remainder 1.

Parallel Lines that are parallel always stay the same distance apart and never meet.

Percentage The proportion or rate per 100 parts.

Perimeter The boundary or edge of an area. The length of the boundary of an area.

Perpendicular A line at right angles to another line.

Pictogram A chart using pictures to represent numbers of items.

Pie chart A circular chart used to illustrate statistical data.

Power The value of a number raised to an exponent, indicating the number of times a number is multiplied by itself.

Primary source Data collected to use for investigation.

Prime A number having only two factors, itself and 1.

Probability The chance an event may happen, given as a fraction, a decimal or a percentage.

Probability scale An ordered line numbered from 0 (the probability of an impossible event) to 1 (the probability of a certain event).

Profit To make money on a deal in business.

Proportion Quantities varying according to a given ratio.

Quadrant One of the four regions of a plane divided by the x-axis and y-axis. Also a part of a circle.

Quadrilaterals Four-sided polygons.

Radius A line joining the centre of a circle to a point on the circumference.

Range The spread of data equal to the difference between the greatest and least values.

Ratio Gives a part to part comparison.

Recurring decimal A decimal fraction with digits that are in a continuous pattern, such as 0.33333.

Reflection The image produced by reflecting an object in an axis of symmetry.

Relative frequency A way of estimating probabilities if they cannot be accurately calculated.

Root A quantity that, when multiplied by itself a certain number of times (once for a square root, twice for a cube root), equals a given amount.

Rotation A shape has rotational symmetry if there are a number of positions the shape can take, when rotated, and still look the same.

Sample A section of a population or a group of observations.

Scale drawing A diagram drawn to a given scale.

Scale factor The ratio of an enlarged distance to the corresponding original value.

Scatter graph A diagram that compares two variables by plotting one value against the other when presented as ordered pairs.

Secondary source Data used for investigation after it has been collected by another party.

Sequence A collection of terms following a rule or pattern.

Similar Figures that are the same shape, but not the same size.

Square number A number that is the product of two equal factors.

Stem-and-leaf diagram A diagram used for displaying grouped data.

Substitute To exchange or replace.

Surface area The total area of the exterior surface.

Tally To count by making marks in groups of five.

Term Part of an expression, equation or sequence.

Terminating decimal A decimal fraction with a finite number of digits.

Theoretical probability Probability predicted using the fraction:

$$\frac{\text{number of particular outcomes that can happen}}{\text{number of outcomes that are possible from the task or event}}$$

Transformation A change made to the position and/or size of a shape.

Translation A transformation in which every point of a shape moves the same distance and direction, as given by a vector.

Triangle Three-sided polygon.

Two-way table A table used to illustrate two variables when organising data.

Variable A quantity, represented by a letter or other symbol, that can take a range of values.

Vector A quantity with size and direction.

Volume The amount of space in a 3D container, measured in cubic millimetres, cubic centimetres or cubic metres.

Answers

What's the point? p5

1 325 pages → 3.25 cm
   25 pages → 2.5 cm

2

Reach for the heights p7

1 a) 13.6, $13\frac{9}{10}$, 14.4, 16, $16\frac{3}{4}$, 20

  b) 12.3, $12\frac{1}{2}$, $13\frac{1}{4}$, 13.4, 14, 15, $15\frac{9}{10}$, 16.1, $17\frac{3}{4}$, 18.1, $20\frac{1}{2}$, 23

2 a) $15\frac{1}{5}$, $15\frac{1}{10}$, 15, $14\frac{2}{3}$, $14\frac{3}{5}$, $14\frac{1}{2}$, $14\frac{3}{10}$, 14, 14, $13\frac{4}{5}$, $13\frac{3}{5}$, $13\frac{1}{5}$

  b) 20, 17, 16.75, 16.7, 16.4, 14, 11.7

3 20.05, 20.075, 20.1, 20.25, 20.275

Pizza topping p9

Common factor

Making a point p13
Match up

1 3.543 21 → 3.54   2.800 16 → 2.80
   2.680 12 → 2.68   1.897 56 → 1.90
   4.037 55 → 4.04   3.689 51 → 3.69
   3.005 55 → 3.01

Fill the gaps

2 a) 1.7, 0.7
   b) 9.4872
   c) they give a realistic measurement
   d) 12.5%
   e) 87.5%
   f) 8.3 m²

Profit or loss? p15

1 £52.43, £54.97, £63.37
2 £55.13
3 a) profit
   b) 25p
   c) 20%
4 a) loss
   b) 15p
   c) 30%

Fishy business p17

1 (i) 1:1:10   (ii) 3:3:35   (iii) 3:3:40
2 (i) N (1 : 2)   (ii) Y   (iii) N (3 : 6 : 4)
   (iv) N (4 : 2 : 1) (v) Y   (vi) N (5 : 2 : 10)
   C
3 Izzy → 8   Nikki → 10   Dan → 14   Jem → 12

Up and down p21

1 car park → −2   cloakroom → −1   coffee → 1   meeting → 4
2 6
3 a) 11.5 m   b) 13.5 m   c) 20 m 35 m   d) 7 m

Happy birthday! p23

1 24
2 a) 5, 10, 15, 20, 25, 30, 35, 40, 45, 50, 55, 60, 65, 70, 75, 80,
       85, 90, 95, 100
   b) 2.24(√5), 3.16(√10), 3.87(√15), 4.47(√20), 5(√25),
       5.48(√30)
3 a) 6   b) 4
4 a) 24   b) 45
5 a) 9   b) 25   c) 5.29   d) 16.81   e) 8   f) 42.875

Which key? p25

1 0.39   0.32   0.322949117
   245   229.84   229.842
   $\frac{3}{7}$ 0.41   0.410958904
   6   6.43   6.431268293

2 (i) $1\frac{1}{8}$ (ii) $1\frac{13}{24}$ (iii) $\frac{23}{4}$ (iv) $4\frac{1}{9}$ (v) 70%   (vi) 55.5%

On the track p29

1 Monday $4c + 3d + 2v$
   Tuesday $3c + 2d + 4v$
   Wednesday $2c + 2d + v$
   Thursday $5c + 2d + 2v$
   Friday $6c + 5d + 4v$
   Monday–Friday $20c + 14d + 13v$
2 sum = $3a$

Translating letters p31

1 °C = 5(°F − 32)/9
2 °F = 9°C/5 + 32
3 0°C → 32°F   5°C → 41°F   15°C → 59°F
   20°C → 68°F   25°C → 77°F   30°C → 86°F
   35°C → 95°F   100°C → 212°F

What is it? p33

1 $10n = 55 → n = 5.5$
2 $2n + 5 = n + 7 → n = 2$
3 Adam 15, Ben 12, Callum 6
4 $x = 30°, y = 60°, z = 90°$
5 $p = 30°, q = 60°, r = 120°, s = 150°$
6 blue 7, brown 21

Which pattern? p37

1

Month	Jan	Feb	Mar	Apr	May	Jun	Jul	Aug	Sep	Oct	Nov	Dec
Number of rabbits	2	2	4	6	10	16	26	42	68	110	178	288

144 pairs

2 a)

Term	1	2	3	4	5	6	7	8	9	10
Squares	1	4	9	16	25	36	49	64	81	100
Matchsticks	4	12	24	40	60	84	112	144	180	220

   b) square   c) difference   difference   4

3 a)

Number of tables	1	2	3	4
Number of pupils	4	6	8	10

   b) adding 2   c) 9

On the straight p39

1 a) $x + y = 4$, b) $y = 4x$, c) $y = -x$, d) $y = 2x + 3$

2

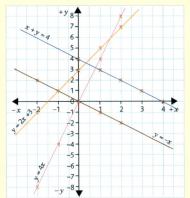

What's the plot? p41

1 a) £15   b) 10p per minute   c) £25   d) 75 minutes
2 a) 6km/h   b) increased   c) 20 minutes   d) stopped

All angles p45

1 a) $p = 45°$ $q = 135°$ $r = 45°$
   b) $g = 55°$ $h = 55°$ $i = 125°$
   c) $x = 65°$ $y = 115°$ $z = 115°$
2 $a_1 = 40°$ $a_2 = 118$ $b_1 = 100°$ $b_2 = 50°$ $c_1 = 20°$ $c_2 = 132°$
   a) sum   b) 180°

Where did the birdie go? p47

1

2 a) 90°   b) 90°   c) 180°
   d) 180°   e) 135°   f) 135°
   g) 180°   h) 45°

3

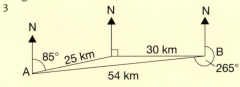

Follow that path p49

1 a)

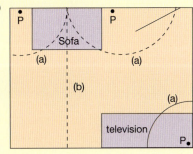

2

3

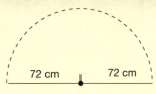

4 a)

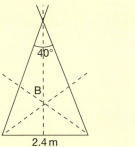

   b) 1.75 m   1.75 m   2.75 m

What a transformation! p53

1 a) 2
   b)

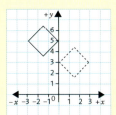

   c)

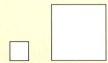

2 a) ISABELLA
      ISABELLA (reflected)
   b) I, B, E unchanged by reflection

How far to go? p55

1 a) 7 ha   b) 1 m²   c) 225 cm²
   d) 8.75 cm²   e) 1.5 m²
2 450 g self raising flour   225 g sugar
   4 tsp ginger   2tsp cinnamon
   225 g margarine   450 g golden syrup
   2 eggs   280 ml milk
   1 tsp bicarbonate of soda
3 a) 10.15 am → 1015
   b) 12.15 am → 0015
   c) 6.35 pm → 1835
   d) 8.20 pm → 2020

Cartons, containers and crates p57

1 Large: 2941.2 cm³/1518 cm²
   Small: 2088 cm³/1249.2 cm²
   Variety: 266.77 cm³/272.22 cm²
2 2134.16 cm³   3 2177.76 cm²
4 25.8 cm × 19 cm × 6 cm   5 variety pack

Turn the tables p61

1 18–25

holiday	tally	frequency
C/C	ЖЖ ЖЖ ЖЖ IIII	19
SC	ЖЖ ЖЖ ЖЖ III	18
B&B	ЖЖ ЖЖ	10
H	III	3

2 families

holiday	tally	frequency
C/C	ЖЖ ЖЖ ЖЖ III	18
SC	ЖЖ ЖЖ ЖЖ ЖЖ	20
B&B	ЖЖ II	7
H	ЖЖ	5

3 55+

holiday	tally	frequency
C/C	ЖЖ III	8
SC	ЖЖ ЖЖ	10
B&B	ЖЖ ЖЖ ЖЖ I	16
H	ЖЖ ЖЖ ЖЖ I	16

2 50, 50, 50 3 primary

4 Internet, other travel firms, newspapers, polls, etc.

What do you mean? p63

1 a) journey times are 1 hour 25 minutes, 1 hour 20 minutes, 1 hour 25 minutes, 1 hour 23 minutes, 1 hour 28 minutes, so the range is 8 mins

b) 1 hour 24 minutes; 1 hour 25 minutes

c) mean   d) 1147, possible delays

2 a) 5.57   b) 6, 6, 5

3 a)

1	8 8
2	2 9 9 9
3	0 5 5 6 7 7 8 9 9
4	0 1 2 3 3 3 4 5 5 5 9
5	0 0 1 2 3 5 5 8 9
6	0 0 0 0 3 4 5 5 7 8
7	0 0 2 2 5 5 8 9
8	0 0 0 3 7 9 0 3

b) 54.5, 52.5, 60

c) mean, all marks are included

Is there a dog in that window? p65

a)
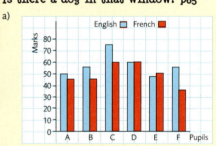

b) generally English marks > French marks

c)
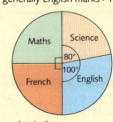

marks similar

d)
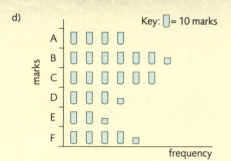

The cost of age p69

1 a) 80€, 160€, 1600€   b) £31.25, £62.50, £125

2

	Weekly allowance	Clothing	Sport	Magazines
Boys	£20	£2.70	£1.50	75p
Girls	£21	£5.30	£1	£1

a) 25%   b) 3/80

Pick a card p71

1 M → $\frac{1}{10}$ A → $\frac{1}{10}$ T → $\frac{1}{10}$ H → $\frac{1}{10}$ S → $\frac{1}{5}$ I → $\frac{1}{10}$ S → $\frac{1}{5}$

F → $\frac{1}{10}$ U → $\frac{1}{10}$ N → $\frac{1}{10}$

a) $\frac{3}{10}$ 0.3 30%   b) $\frac{1}{2}$ 0.6 60%

2 a)   Probability of picking favourite from:

	Chococrunch	Chocomix
Friend A	$\frac{5}{12}$	$\frac{1}{3}$
Friend B	$\frac{1}{4}$	$\frac{7}{24}$
Friend C	$\frac{1}{3}$	$\frac{3}{8}$

b) Chococrunch

Take a chance p73

1 a) $\frac{24}{49}$ b) $\frac{15}{49}$ c) $\frac{10}{49}$

   d) $\frac{1}{7}$ e) $\frac{4}{49}$

2 a) 0.13

3 a) theoretical probability   b) secondary data

   c) secondary data   d) experiment

   e) experiment